DATE DUE

~~5-13-03~~			
9-13-12			

Demco No. 62-0549

ADVERTISING AND SOCIAL CHANGE

The SAGE CommText Series

Editor:
F. GERALD KLINE
*Director, School of Journalism and Mass Communication
University of Minnesota*

Associate Editor:
SUSAN H. EVANS
Department of Communication, University of Michigan

This new series of communication textbooks is designed to provide a modular approach to teaching in this rapidly changing area. The explosion of concepts, methodologies, levels of analysis, and philosophical perspectives has put heavy demands on teaching undergraduates and graduates alike; it is our intent to choose the most solidly argued of these to make them available for students and teachers. The addition of new titles in the CommText series as well as the presentation of new and diverse authors will be a continuing effort on our part to reflect change in this scholarly area.

—F.G.K. and S.H.E.

Ronald Berman

ADVERTISING
AND
SOCIAL CHANGE

Volume 8. **The Sage COMMTEXT Series**

 SAGE PUBLICATIONS   Beverly Hills   London

For information address:

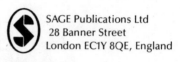

SAGE Publications, Inc.
275 South Beverly Drive
Beverly Hills, California 90212

SAGE Publications Ltd
28 Banner Street
London EC1Y 8QE, England

Printed in the United States of America

Library of Congress Cataloging in Publication Data

Berman, Ronald.
   Advertising and social change.

   (The Sage commtext series ; v. 8)
   Bibliography: p.
   1. Advertising — Social aspects — United States.
I. Title.   II. Series.
HF5813.U6B39   659.1'042'0973   81-14326
ISBN 0-8039-1737-6   AACR2
ISBN 0-8039-1738-4 (pbk.)

SECOND PRINTING, 1982

FOR

KATHY, JULIE, AND ANDREW

CONTENTS

ACKNOWLEDGMENTS

I am grateful to the John M. Olin Foundation, which made the writing of this book possible. That gratitude extends particularly to its Executive Director, Michael S. Joyce. Parts of the following appeared in the 50th anniversary edition of *Advertising Age*, and I have benefited greatly from talks with the Chairman of its Executive Committee, Sid Bernstein, and with Stanley E. Cohen, its Washington editor. I would also like to thank those who were kind enough to let me interview them.

I think that such a society is always on the move and that none of its members knows what rest is; but I think that all bestir themselves within certain limits which they hardly ever pass. Daily they change, alter, and renew things of secondary importance, but they are very careful not to touch fundamentals. They love change, but they are afraid of revolutions.

It is very difficult to make the inhabitants of democracies listen when one is not talking about themselves.

Alexis de Tocqueville, "Why Great Revolutions Will Become Rare," *Democracy in America.*

PREFACE

On the 50th anniversary of *Advertising Age* I was asked to contribute an essay to a special edition devoted to advertising's affect on society. That essay, on advertising and social change, opened so many issues about a particular industry and its place in American culture that a full-scale study seemed appropriate. Advertising in itself is the subject of many books; and as for social change, that is now an unavoidable part of most of our national debates. I know that more could be written about the relationship of advertising to social change, and I trust that it will. Perhaps future books will refer to this one.

I have not tried to exhaust the issue: This book is for the most part about advertising and television. Nor have I tried to give full historical coverage to the industry: That has been done already. This book is a limited attempt to make certain statements about our conception of change.

The first and introductory chapter is about advertising and its critics. Its purpose is to indicate the extent to which criticism is organized around ideas about a good society, about productivity, or about the existential necessities. The next chapter is about critical method. It examines theories of social control and covers ways of evaluating television in general and advertising in particular.

The third chapter suggests a prehistory for advertising. It argues that if we are to judge from literary and historical example, advertising has often shaped our cultural imagination. And it suggests also that advertising now defines middle-class expectations. Its most consistent message is not that goods and services satisfy, but that consumption defines mass society.

Chapter 4 is necessarily the longest because it takes up questions about that mass society. This part of the book deals with the ways in which ideas of social change are transmitted. Its argument is that televised commercials depict the American family and community in predictable ways. Advertising maneuvers between nostalgia and hunger for the satisfactions of the future. It is capable of painting life in two entirely contradictory ways: (1) organized around a kind of society at least one generation out of date and (2) promising a kind of individuality free of any social conscience.

The last topic is government, or rather bureaucracy. Chapter 5 examines the stated purposes of certain federal agencies and the social changes they recommend.

Perhaps the most fascinating subject for Americans to consider is themselves. And, in an age like ours, that subject is bound to be approached through the fact of social change. We worry endlessly about the relationship of present to future. We never tire of thinking about what we have been and about what we may become. These great themes of the imagination, once in the province of literature, have now become part of advertising. The fact is that advertising does much more than persuade us to consume goods and services: It tells us who we are.

Advertisements, especially on television, have become vignettes of social life. They portray individuals with many social relationships. They suggest ways of dealing with those relationships — of living among friends, parents, and fellow employees. They give us a great deal of advice about work, maturation, marriage, and other aspects of social life. Above all, they give us information about living that life in conditions of incessant change.

Change is not easy to experience. We all know that we must age — but few of us are eager for that to happen. We all know that we must constrain individual freedom: As Freud wrote in *Civilization and Its Discontents,* social history is the history of restraint. But there are ever fewer guides to our situation. The institutions of family, religion, and education have grown noticeably weaker over each of the past three generations. The world itself seems to have grown more complex. In the absence of traditional authority, advertising has become a kind of social guide. It depicts us in all the myriad situations possible to a life of free choice. It provides ideas about style, morality, behavior. It is especially concerned to describe human relationships: between one individual and another, between individuals and institutions. In so doing, advertising acts as more than a guide to consumption. The following pages examine what is essentially a new kind of American social institution, one which is very much with us, and very much in need of criticism and understanding. In brief, *Advertising and Social Change* is about the contemporary critique of advertising and about advertising's affect on mass middle-class culture.

1

ADVERTISING AND THE RATIONAL STATE

More than we realize, the criticism of advertising involves the criticism of other things. It may be organized around the idea of a good society, around the desirability of productivity, even around the difference between our needs and our desires. This chapter is about the different ways in which modern economists, philosophers, and psychologists have approached the problem of evaluating advertising's affect on our social lives.

THE VOICE OF TECHNOLOGY

For half a century the standard of living in America has climbed steadily — spectacularly — upward. We now have longer life expectancies, more opportunity for education, and new fields of employment. The change in longevity has been unique in human history. White males born in 1930 could expect to live for 60 years and black males for only 48: expectations by 1974, according to the U.S. Department of Commerce (1977: 190-191) publication *Social Indicators 1976*, were for the former about 68 and for the latter about 63. The credit for this is due both to immunology and antibacterial treatment and to the conditions of industrial life such as improved nutrition, hygiene, and public welfare. *Social Indicators* adds that blacks and whites were, when classified by family income, "about equally likely to be attending some kind of postsecondary school in the early 1970's"(1977: 260). As for employment, there has been a redefinition of work in our part of the 20th century, with benefits, security, and working conditions for the mass exceeding the dreams of either Victorian or socialist reform.

Whether we judge by these changes or by increased leisure, ownership, income, or social participation, it is indisputable that our material lives have changed. They have been affected by one of the most powerful of modern forces: productivity. But that productivity is silent if not, as Joseph Schumpeter (1975) has written, ineloquent in its own defense. In order to be heard it must rely on advertising. Advertising has diffused information about commodities, marketed them, and persuaded us of their place in our lives. It has done substantially more than this. When we think about the use of television for commercials we are really thinking of the role advertising plays in social change. It celebrates change. It internalizes change for the woman who becomes better (or simply better looking) by using a certain product or service. Advertising is the voice of technology: Because of that it represents the intention to affect life.

Technology, despite our ambiguous feelings about it, is ingrained in Western culture. Its presence may be felt in Wordsworth's lines on Westminster Bridge about the sight of "Ships, towers, domes, theatres, and temples" equalling the power of the natural world to affect the human heart. As he put it, "Earth has not anything to show more fair" (quoted in Hutchinson, 1953: 214). It may be that London and all other cities have lost that capacity, but our cultural imagination, to judge by movies, books, and myths, is still focused on factory, highway, and city and on the new social order they imply. The novels of Dickens are exciting because they depict a new realm of human activity for his readers. His institutions are banks, courts, factories, and the new bourgeois household adapted to deal (or fail to deal) with them. Some novels, like *Hard Times*, are about the infernal aspects of industrial life: its slums, poverty, and resentment. But others, like *David Copperfield* and *Great Expectations*, see the new realm in terms of opportunity and even in terms of freedom.[1] The rise of Oliver Twist to middle-class affluence is the object of his story. Perhaps Lionel Trilling said it best when he called the great theme of modern fiction The Rise of the Young Man from the Provinces. The figure of the man who "rises" to social power is at the heart of Stendhal's works and those of Dickens and Fitzgerald.[2]

The rise to power and tragic knowledge often implies a fall. From the early 19th century on, our feelings about technology have been ambiguous. Blake wrote about factories which were in every sense of the term *satanic*, while Frank Lloyd Wright could conceive of a technology almost entirely liberating. In Hart Crane's *The Bridge*, industrialism has its own aesthetic:

> The nasal whine of power whips a new universe . . .
> Where spouting pillars spoor the evening sky,
> Under the looming stacks of the gigantic power house
> Stars prick the eyes with sharp ammoniac proverbs,
> New verities, new inklings in the velvet hummed
> Of dynamos . . . [1970: 41].

It is not that technology is a blessing but that, as Crane perceives, it is a new verity of life. And all understood verities are exciting.

There are various kinds of technology, but the one we are most familiar with is directed at everyday life. The social history of that life is more humble than the history of politics, war, or diplomacy. But it matters a great deal for those who experience it. Ben Wattenberg's (1976) book *The Real America* argues that the common use of the washing machine and automatic dryer has had more to do with the new relationship of men and women than any

ideology of liberation. It has removed one of the traditional curses of occupation. When he reminds us of
what it was like taking in frozen wash on a winter's day, we
may agree that a labor-saving device can be existentially
far more than a convenience. Technological change on this
level has given us longer lives and arguably better ones. It
might at least be put that it has provided more choice for
this generation than for any preceding it.

Technology must be communicated: It is one thing to
invent a machine but another to make it a national institution. The role of advertising has been to mediate between
technology and the marketplace. To the extent that it has
fulfilled this role, it has shared in credit and responsibility
for the accomplishments of the economy.

But social change is more than economic, and certainly
more than an automatic sequence of improvements.
Many of the changes that society undergoes turn out to be
disappointments: More education may be worse education; higher income may mean only that work is profitable,
not that it is satisfying. If the 1980s are like the 1970s, then
rewards may become less important than what we now
call "self-fulfillment."

Our view of social life sometimes does not correspond
to economic improvement, only to our expectations. *Public Opinion*, the bimonthly survey of poll-taking in the
United States, indicates the measureable degree of national dissatisfaction with taxation, inflation, government,
law, leadership, foreign affairs, and many other issues
within the public realm (see "Opinion roundup, 1979a,
1979b). If there is a central theme to those dissatisfactions,
it is disappointment in institutions. We think less of government than we used to and a great deal less of media.
Advertising is necessarily involved in that disappointment
because it speaks so directly about values within the public realm. Insofar as it is perceived to express ideas or

morals or beliefs, it shares a place with other institutions in our suspicions.

It is difficult, perhaps impossible, to lavish praise upon a product for 60 seconds and still keep the viewer's attention. A very common strategy of advertising has been to associate a given product with human experience: to suggest that its use is connected to a happy family life or a good education or a decent job. The assumption is that we feel good about being middle class or simply about being American and that we will relate the use of that product to our feelings. But a new audience comes along everyday, with a new set of social values. Today's audience may define responsible middle-class life in terms of moral restraint rather than in terms of material improvement.

TECHNOLOGY AND THE GOOD LIFE

A general theory has, indeed, appeared which views productivity as the cause of Western moral and cultural decline. Its contours are familiar: limiting consumption, ending dependence upon raw materials, and changing from an industrial to an agrarian style of life. Modern civilization has many discontents. As Joseph Schumpeter (1975: 129) said in *Capitalism, Socialism and Democracy*, "it does not follow that men are 'happier' or even 'better off' in the industrial society of today than they were in a medieval manor or village." But, he added something equally worth pondering: "Mankind is not free to choose. . . . Things economic and social move by their own momentum and the ensuing situations compel individuals and groups to behave in certain ways whatever they may wish to do."

In some fundamental ways the criticism of advertising is about the nature of industrial life. In the view of social

rationalism we are in fact not better off under an un-
limited, unregulated, and unsanctified form of productivity. Whatever promotes that system is morally
suspect. Oddly enough, that view is not shared by those
most in need of a modern economy. Peter Drucker has
written in *The Age of Discontinuity* about the view of
undeveloped societies:

> If people cannot yet afford an automobile, they will at
> least get a motor scooter; and if they cannot afford a
> motor scooter, they will try for a bicycle. For the masses
> of the world, radio and TV are not "entertainment" — as
> they are for the wealthy who have other means to learn
> about the world. They are the first access to a bigger
> world than that of peasant village or small-town slum
> [1978: 78].

Advertising is perceived by those primitive economies to
be the symbol of change and to speak for productivity
which is the entry into modern life.

The success of our own economy allows us to reject at
least the *idea* of affluence. A number of things — among
them the expansion of government and the opening up of
"policy" as a field for intellectuals — have revived the
Platonic idea of the rational state. As John Kenneth Galbraith (1971: 337) has put it, "the educational and scientific
estate" can be expected to have more and more weight in
national discourse. The rational state that is so often conceived by this New Class has these characteristics:

(1) It believes in the restraint of irresponsible corporate
enterprise. Corporations, especially the multinationals,
are too large, too inefficient, too self-serving — and far
too immune to social criticism.

(2) The truly rational state will restrain unnecessary productivity. We do not need much of what we produce;
and in any case we are guilty of wasting many of the
world's resources.

(3) Planning is or should be a central activity: connecting the realm of intellectuals with the *metier* of economics.

(4) Consumption will in the rational state become completely redefined. Material satisfactions are to be replaced by psychological satisfactions.

(5) Finally, equality is in the rational state a moral as well as economic end. The distribution of all satisfactions, including income, should aim at equality.

Galbraith has been particularly concerned with what he perceives to be advertising's inutility. It is important to recall the central place of advertising in Galbraith's view of economics as a whole: It matters so much because it has invalidated the classical idea of supply and demand. Many economists believe that the free market responds to supply and demand, but in fact demand is artificially induced for the sake of ever-greater sales and profits. The guilt of advertising resides in its encouragement of unnecessary production that wastes resources — and that has undesirable affects upon social character.

Galbraith's (1976: 124-139) *The Affluent Society* is really about "the good society" which might come into being by a process of cultural displacement. In the good society our desires would not be artificial. We would consume much less. We would be politically and personally altruistic. And we would be free of the most obtrusive of all modern things, the creation of desire. Tactically, we would be free of advertising, which is the cause of those desires.

In a lengthening series of books, Galbraith has referred to economics in order to explain advertising and has gone well beyond economics to characterize it. He has, with differing success, written about psychology, aesthetics, and philosophy. As we look over these books, beginning with *The Affluent Society,* we are struck by their declarative reasoning and by the given assumptions to which they refer themselves. *The Affluent Society* is a book of the

1960s, with a view of human nature dependent on a liberal consensus. It accepts, without a great deal of evidence, that corporations are against individuals; that businessmen need the guidance of intellectuals; that a principal datum for social change is the interest of the younger generation in environmental protection. Even later editions of *The Affluent Society* fail to acknowledge that a social sensibility may itself be subject to change. It was an article of faith in the 1960s that those enrolled in college were altruistic, intelligent, and sublimely politically aware. This was ascribed to the natural idealism of youth. By 1976, when the book went into its third edition, the young were being criticized for their obsession with careers, success, and other benefits of productivity. The same critics were often the source of both *laus et vituperatio*.

There are some logical difficulties with the central matter of created demand. The bulk of advertising's budget goes into household items like soap, food, and automobiles. The five leading advertisers for 1978 were Proctor & Gamble, General Foods, American Home Products Corporation, General Mills, and General Motors. They spent enormous amounts of money (approximately $1 billion in 1978) but on a very limited range of products. They did not promote more than a fraction of those products displayed on Fifth Avenue between 49th and 57th Streets. Mass advertising sticks fairly closely to the large market for necessities. If it were in fact possible to create demand, then the model for our economy might become *The New Yorker* rather than commercial television. The upper middle class, liberated by taste, education, and income, uses more unadvertised goods like antiques and more unadvertised services like restaurants than those whose world is more circumscribed. Indulgence may well be a function of social class and disposable income.

In *The New Industrial State*, Galbraith discusses advertising under the unpropitious heading of "The Industrial System and the Cold War." It is here that he identifies corporate advertising with government propaganda: "Management involves the creation of a compelling image of the product in the mind of the consumer. . . . Fantasy and image-building also play an important role in the relationship between the industrial system and the state" (1971: 328). Government observes the producer falsifying claims in order to make profits and it learns to falsify reality so that citizens will conform to its policies. It invents a Soviet menace so that an army will be maintained. It invents domestic and foreign crises so that industry will be relieved of regulation. In *The New Industrial State* the techniques of advertising are used by institutions against people.

Advertising offends more than values: from the viewpoint of the rational state, it promotes the preference for goods over leisure, for productivity over the rights of the environment, and for "the unqualified commitment to technological change" (Galbraith, 1971: 345). The rational state prefers a steady rather than an expanding economy — and moral rather than technological change. Consumption is more than a vice, more than one of the seven material sins. As Galbraith reminds us, the view of social order conveyed by advertising, with all its suggestions of indulgence and plenitude, is wrong, false, and opposite to his own. Every advertisement that appears must in his terms be an obstacle to the creation of a rational state of mind, let alone a rational polity. That is why, in books devoted to the analysis of the economic system, advertising bulks so large — why it is his *bête noire*. Galbraith and his followers attack advertising not because it is inherently dislikable but because it symbolizes productivity. The impression of peasant societies as described above by

Drucker seems to be entirely right: They are hypnotized by television because of the message, not the medium.

In *The New Industrial State* then, the argument of *The Affluent Society* has been carried a good deal further, from an essentially moral to an essentially political conclusion, But, certain problems have not been addressed: Psychological evidence for the sameness of our fantasies and our foreign policy never appears, nor does philosophical evidence for the relationship of advertising to social immorality. Later books have not advanced the argument. Although *Economics and the Public Purpose* states that it forms a triad along with the two earlier works, it tends, on the subject of advertising, to summarize their generalities. Galbraith is ingenious and interesting when he guesses at the motives of producers and of the "technostructure" formed by industry and government. But he does leave to others the evidence for the case that in America we now have "management of the private consumer" (see Galbraith, 1973: 137).[3]

Galbraith has, however, made some important contributions to the critique of advertising, whether right or wrong. Before his work, discourse tended to see advertising largely in terms of *The Hidden Persuaders:* as an interesting moral deviation in marketing. The criticism of advertising had no intellectual base; it was obsessed with the lesser forms of indignation. After Galbraith it was difficult to perceive advertising simply as marketing and likely to perceive it as an affirmation of capitalist ideology. Second, the new critique of advertising based itself upon the idea of the rational state. A theory of human nature and the good social life arose which self-consciously attacked traditional middle-class values. Third, with a great deal of precision (although with much less accuracy) the great fault of advertising was judged to be its worship of productivity and consumption in an age of scarcity. And fourth, there was a redefinition of critical terms and method. We now have what is very nearly a discipline devoted to the reification of Galbraith's assumptions.

THE PSYCHOLOGY OF CONSUMPTION

Clearly, Galbraith is not solely responsible for the enormous literary output on the sin of productivity and the vice of consumption. There has been a good deal of original work complementing his own, for example, that of Herbert Marcuse. Marcuse and Galbraith were possibly the two most influential cultural figures of the 1960s. And I think it can be said that their work was mutually reinforcing: *One-Dimensional Man* has provided some of the aesthetic and philosophical answers for the questions raised by *The Affluent Society*.

Here is how *One-Dimensional Man* begins its investigation of consumption:

> The people recognize themselves in their commodities; they find their soul in their automobile, hi-fi set, split-level home, kitchen equipment. The very mechanism which ties the individual to his society has changed [Marcuse, 1964: 9].

The point is arguable, but I think that there are two kinds of truth it displays. The first is that American middle-class life is indeed characterized by possessions; the second, that some of those possessions have powerful symbolic meanings. Differences of opinion arise when we think of the depth of attachment we have for our possessions — and of the power that their producers may be said to have over us. For Marcuse as for Galbraith, productivity is a conspiracy. But Marcuse has gone much further in his analysis of consumption. While Galbraith was content to assert that happiness will supposedly be "enhanced in proportion as more goods are produced and consumed" (1973: 140), Marcuse added that our "civilization transforms the object world into an extension of man's mind and body" (1964: 9).

Marcuse, in short, provided a theory of "true and false needs" (see 1964: 4-18) which were only implied in the writings of Galbraith. In a rather impatient way, Galbraith had suggested that middle-class *taste* was excessive: his opinion of middle-class life was stylistic, viewing it *de haut en bas*. Marcuse put the matter in terms of specific psychological consequences. As he saw it, the economic system provided false emotional satisfactions: "to behave and consume in accordance with the advertisements" (1964: 5) was to degrade human consciousness.

One-Dimensional Man states the theme of cultural repression. *Satisfaction is a form of that repression.* This is not so paradoxical as it may appear: Since the advent of the psychoanalytical method, it has been conventional to reason from opposites. All unconscious activity hides its real meaning, and interpretation proceeds by unmasking and by reversal. Only dreams tell the truth — even the discourse of children deludes our censorship. The peculiar genius of industrialism, according to Marcuse, has been to provide substitutes for the natural desires of the unconscious. There is, for example, the powerful fact of sexual desire. We all need — and must have — sexual fulfillment. But what we get is a culture that sublimates nature: ads full of naked women which convert love into consumption.

It is no exaggeration to say that advertising has the same central place in Marcuse that it has in Galbraith. Here are two passages from *One-Dimensional Man:* the first about advertising in general and the second about its sexual sublimation:

> The irresistible output of the entertainment and information industry carry with them prescribed attitudes

and habits, certain intellectual and emotional reactions which bind the consumers more or less pleasantly to the producers and, through the latter, to the whole. The products indoctrinate and manipulate; they promote a false consciousness which is immune against its falsehood [1964: 12].

The body is allowed to exhibit its sexual features in the everyday work world and in work relations. This is one of the unique achievements of industrial society — rendered possible by the reduction of dirty and heavy physical labor; by the availability of cheap, attractive clothing, beauty culture, and physical hygiene; by the requirements of the advertising industry, etc. [1964: 74].

The first passage criticizes more than the profit motive. Galbraith had in *The Affluent Society* decried productivity because of its misallocation; Marcuse sees it as a form of political bribery. It keeps mass society in a state of dull acquiescence. The phrase "false consciousness" does not refer to the conventional Marxian meaning of mistaking a historical situation: It means here the loss of psychological awareness. Consumption — literally — displaces sexuality in favor of lesser pleasures.

Both passages assume that advertisements are irresistible, that products force us to love them, and that the system is immune to criticism. The distribution of guilt is interesting because it is suggested that while the good things of life like love and sexuality are transcendent, we are not responsible for failing to do them justice. The social-economic system is guilty of that, human nature being responsible only for its weakness. Its interpretation of man is that he is a creature with very nearly divine powers of experience — but without the moral restraint to use them. Human nature simply reacts.

But we have, after all, been reared on these assumptions. For several decades in American life desires have become defined as needs, and anything opposing them has tended to lose its legitimacy. At any rate, Marcuse has isolated the psychological consequences of industrialism, to his own satisfaction. He has identified the agency responsible for "controlled desublimation," that is, for causing passive social conformity by converting normal sexual feelings into the desire to consume. Advertising, hitherto criticized for its vulgarity and materialism, for being a barrier to entry or simply the mainstay of commercial television, is the mode by which industrial society enforces its will. It allows the underlying unhappiness of our civilization to forget itself in the contemplation of plastic nudity.

We have a long history of the criticism of consumption, going back to the works of Veblen and beyond. But I think it can be said with no exaggeration that modern polemics on advertising and social change derive from Galbraith and Marcuse. Nearly all succeeding writers combine the two arguments that productivity is an economic evil and consumption, a psychological evil.

The two arguments have been assimilated into discourse and have now all the advantages of dogma. Books like *Economic Thought and Social Change* by J. Ron Stanfield or *Captains of Consciousness* by Stuart Ewen assume that it is no longer necessary to prove the point. Stanfield, for example, has written of "truly human needs" that are nothing less — or more — than "meaningful participation in sexual intercourse, a sense of belonging to a human community, a feeling of potency" (1979: 67). These are interesting, but not what philosophy has labored over since the Platonic dialogues defined the good life. They are not what King Lear described (in terms that might almost win the approval of Milton Friedman) as the basic necessities of "raiment, bed, and food."

To make sexuality the measure of needs is to assume that it is both rational and consistent. But it is neither — at least if we can believe this *locus classicus* from Euripides:

I pray that love may never come to me
with murderous intent,
in rhythms measureless and wild [Lattimore, 1959: 185].

These lines are terrifying. The error of social rationalism, in respect to love at least, has been to confuse it with conscience, hence with the realm of politics. As for the de facto decision to define needs out of existence, something has in fact been written about that:

O, reason not the need! Our basest beggars
Are in the poorest things superfluous.
Allow not nature more than nature needs,
Man's life is cheap as beasts [Kittredge, 1936: 1216].

Desires tend to resist political theory.

Literature is sometimes as informative as economics: Pygmalion had a "meaningful" sexual relationship with a statue; Narcissus had one with his own reflection; and, if Shakespeare is to be trusted, the Dauphin of France had one with his horse. It is fairly hopeless to make sexuality a standard when its nature implies an infinity of satisfactions. It is quite literally hopeless to confuse the sexual with the normative — for every happy adjustment of Encounter or Gestalt or Awareness Weekends there is a page of Kraft-Ebbing that will curl your hair. And it is, if not hopeless, somewhat ingenuous to blame advertising for the vagaries of nature. We must, in fact, "desublimate" sexuality ourselves; at least if we are to believe Freud:

It is impossible to overlook the extent to which civilization is built up upon a renunciation of instinct, how much it presupposes precisely the non-satisfaction (by suppression, repression or some other means?) of powerful instincts. This "cultural frustration" dominates the large field of social relationships between human beings [1961: 44].

There are other points to be made by rationalism, and certainly *Economic Thought and Social Change* tries to operate on as broad a front as possible. Here is a sample of Stanfield's thought on the relationship of advertising to other cultural modes:

> Beneath the appeal of such manipulative phenomena as advertising and blind patriotism is alienation [1979: 67].

> Deprived of active modes for self-expression, they respond to the fantastic associations of ad men, politicos, rabble rousers, and clergy [1979: 67].

> The false need for the commodity may pacify for the moment, but it cannot satisfy. The need will return again and again [1979: 68].

The first two passages are about guilt by association: The phrase "ad men, politicos, rabble rousers, and clergy" is a kind of multiple synonym for the illegitimacy of commerce, government, and religion. Advertising is the occasion for resentment, while the major attack is upon those social circumstances which advertising represents. As for the third passage, it refers to what, in both economics and psychology, used to be referred to as the law of diminishing returns. The irritation of this particular passage refers not entirely to the attractions of commodities but to the vagaries of human nature. In the rational state, our feelings will be different.

The Ewen book is very much a descendant of Marcuse's *One-Dimensional Man*. It is inferior to the original, but full of representative qualities. The idea of repression has become far more general and inclusive since Marcuse wrote, and this book has assimilated many of the ideas of the therapeutic movement. By now, words like "authoritarian" and "repressive" are being used as if the political realm and that of emotional experience were identical. Whatever contributes to a sense of personal unease — even to the "atmosphere" of society — has no legitimacy. This goes beyond the sexual desublimation of Marcuse, and even beyond Adorno, Horkheimer, Wilhelm Reich, and those others who have formulated for our time a vision of innocent man and guilty social institutions.

Captains of Consciousness expresses the Grand Strategy of social rationalism, its total view of our civilization. There is a complete orchestration (possible only to science and to fanaticism) of every problem or failing in American life: the Great Depression, the Cold War, the plight of minorities, even the trial of Julius and Ethel Rosenberg. These things are attributed to the power of advertising. There is "a politics of daily life" (Ewen, 1976: 219) for which corporations are responsible. They not only seduce us with commodities but also, in a Pavlovian way, condition us to believe that there are no other rewards in life or other sources for those rewards. And, since corporations become identified with what they produce, they take on all the psychic authority once associated with God, family, or nature.

In short, advertising exists not to sell commodities, but to praise the name of corporations. It takes our minds off the injustice of the social order and prevents us from seeing that it should be replaced.

Stanfield is insistent about the validity of the critique leveled against American life (and against its liberal defenders) by the New Left. And it seems that his theory of advertising is a revised form of theories popular in the 1960s about another social agency. Advertising now seems to serve the same purpose that education served from the occupation of the Bancroft Strip to the bombing of the

University of Wisconsin. Education and advertising both subsist on literacy. Universities, which were easily among the most liberal and tolerant of social institutions in the 1960s (as they are now), were perceived by the New Left to be among the most wicked. It was their function that mattered: their articulation of habits, beliefs, procedures, and values. About half the cohort from 18 to 21 attended college of some kind, at some time or another; and the agency that oversaw their socialization was necessarily the object of radical criticism. The other half of that age cohort may slip through the net of education, but they cannot avoid that of mass culture. Advertising socializes individuals in a way that roughly resembles education, providing them with ideas, images, and examples of cultural expectations. It must be as guilty as any other kind of social agency if it can be proved that we are learning the wrong things.

IMPOSSIBLE DESIRES

This rather unsparing summary of social rationalism is not intended to denigrate. There are a number of works that it has produced which have to be taken seriously. I have tried to give some representative coverage, to show the intellectual basis of Galbraith and of Marcuse, and to show some derivations and additions in Ewen and Stanfield. Another pair of books shows the critique of advertising and social change to be capable of a good deal more. Christopher Lasch's *The Culture of Narcissism* has had mixed reviews, but I think its analysis of advertising, although harsh, deserves more attention than it has received. And *The Limits to Satisfaction,* by William Leiss, is a very serious work about those social redefinitions which will have to be made before guilt for the failures of our social order is confidently ascribed.

The Culture of Narcissism begins with the premise that self-awareness is now both a condition and a commodity. It then makes the following points, in an argument which is I think consecutive and at least partially convincing:

(1) Mass production demands a mass market. And, in the words of Edward A. Filene in 1919, "the masses must learn to behave like human beings in a mass production world."

(2) Civilizing the masses means giving them certain ideas. Among those ideas is what Calvin Coolidge described as "the desire . . . for better things," implied by advertising.

(3) The original function served by advertising was marketing products. Now, unfortunately, it serves to market feelings, sensations and styles of life. It suggests not that a product works, but that consumption will cure the problems of age, sex, or loneliness.

(4) In so doing, advertising becomes part of the spiritual cant of the age. It feeds on alienation and addresses not needs, but personal dissatisfactions.

(5) Advertising has two faces: One serves the powers that be; the other tries to utilize the astounding "revolution in manners and morals" that we have undergone in the twentieth century. One thing is perhaps as bad as another, for when advertising allies itself with the sexual revolution it succeeds only in destroying social authority; when it encourages the liberation of women it only sets the sexes against each other; when it flatters the young and glorifies youth it makes mature social expectations impossible [1978: 72].

It can be seen that Lasch differs significantly from the utopian social rationalists. He values customs and traditions and those institutions which sustain them. He is not especially anxious to commit the moral authority for social life to the power of the state. He finds that many things taken seriously by social rationalism — for example, the ceaseless movement of both mass and elite culture toward personal liberation — can be morally and emotionally destructive. While advertising is most often attacked as a *conserving* social force, he perceives its own revolutionism:

> The "education" of the masses has altered the balance of forces within the family, weakening the authority of the husband in relation to the wife and parents in relation to their children. It emancipates women and children from patriarchal authority, however, only to subject them to the new paternalism of the advertising industry, the industrial corporation, and the state [Lasch, 1978: 74].

Advertising, so often accused of being a bulwark of capitalism, may in fact be a kind of Trojan Horse. Far from preserving social inertia, as its critics on the left so often adduce, it becomes a carrier of anxiety. It suggests dissatisfaction with the way we live and with what we are. As Lasch sees it, our culture is now marked by an exaggerated form of self-awareness, a kind of mass narcissism. All things are judged by the demands of the narcissistic self. And advertising, in recognizing those demands, displays on every television screen a universal emotional type: self-absorbed, self-righteous, dependent on the momentary pleasures of assertion. Advertising becomes the medium of alienation.

The Limits to Satisfaction is complex and ambiguous. Although it shares with much of social rationalism the premise that we are consuming our way through the world's resources, and the conviction that consumption is psychologically induced, it has few easy answers. Leiss begins by abandoning the idea that we can distinguish between "true" and "false" needs or that self-constituted authorities can do that for us. Some things that have long been considered to be "needs" by those in favor of increasing the power of the state seem to have no reference either to actual desires or to realistic standards. What is the good of "bulk foodstuffs for the poor" or of "the drab uniformity of public housing projects" and other measures dreamed of by the bureaucracies of the welfare state (Leiss, 1976: 63)? Needs have qualitative aspects that are too often invisible to reform. Among them are beauty, comfort, and intelligibility.

This book is impartially analytical and suggests that there have been errors on both sides of our social dialogue. According to Leiss, there are four essential problems for a society based upon the circulation of commodities:

(1) When advertising suggests that the taste of menthol in a cigarette is like the advent of springtime, it makes both ends of the comparison incoherent. Human experience becomes fragmented, and our responses are made to unworthy and unintelligible objects.

(2) Consumption destabilizes society. Advertisements associate commodities with qualities that have largely disappeared from social life like "quiet and serenity, open space, and closeness to the natural environment."[4] They evoke craftsmanship, unspoiled wilderness, close family life, and any number of other things that the industrialized market economy has caused to disappear. This causes an intolerable ambiguity in public life as we are forced to associate what we get (which is always new, always changing, and always trivial) with what we have given up to get it.

(3) We become indifferent to quality. A world of individual nuances, of beauty to be found in the differences of wood grain or in the colors of fabric, is lost to us because of mass production and false satisfaction of mere novelty.

(4) The environmental risks of a commodity-based economy are unacceptably high. Nature must become a part of our economic calculations and its preservation

recognized as one of the very few genuine needs of existence.

Much of this is arguable, which is acknowledged by the author. He does not have a panacea for the change of social customs by the prior change of human nature. He has little confidence in the powers of the state to improve our minds. He suggests that abundance is deceptive and that it breeds dissatisfactions. And he urges, as a beginning to dialogue, that we rethink the categories of the necessary and the desirable.

Even within the school of thought that I have called social rationalism there are many differences of opinion. But it is useful, before discussing advertising and social change, to see what definitions may be involved. There are different versions of both advertising and of social change: *Captains of Consciousness* states that "social change cannot come about" (Ewen, 1976: 220) while advertising persists, and *The Culture of Narcissism* states that advertising destabilizes human relationships almost daily. For many critics, advertising is a secondary preoccupation. They are interested in it as a contingency of production, consumption, and the utilization of resources. Arguments have been addressed which are bewildering in their variety: that consumption displaces sexuality, that advertising is a kind of licensed pornography, and that it either sustains or undermines the powers of capitalist culture.

A good deal more remains to be said, because this critical dialogue eventually finds its way into media, government, and other branches of the social sciences. Behaviorism, for example, almost unconsciously accepts certain premises when it begins to catalogue the "fairness" of television, premises about the desirability of changing society so that we will become more healthy, less prejudiced, or more peaceful. It works these premises into the texture of seemingly independent discussion, especially of the convoluted issues of sex and violence on television. The critical dialogue that I have sketched finds its ways into courtrooms as well as into universities.

If the "real" issues are sometimes hard to grasp, they are perhaps not so hard to see. When the FTC was reviewed by *U.S. News & World Report* in 1979 it quoted the following:

> Samuel Thurm, senior vice president of the Association of National Advertisers, retorts: "The real issue is the changing of society. What the regulators would like to do is have society behave differently — drive slower, eat less, not smoke, be nicer people" [Lang, 1979: 31].

The "real issue" in regulating advertising may have more to do with psychology than with marketing. Social change inevitably means that present social arrangements are compared with an idea of what Galbraith (and many others, in a long line extending back to the Platonic dialogues) have called "the good society." Perhaps the matter was put best, with a sardonic and heavy hand, by the *Wall Street Journal* in 1978: "Anyone who could . . . invest heavy personal resources of time and attention to launch a frontal assault on Frosted Flakes and Boo Berries has got to have a sense of the moral order of this world that is — to put it delicately — a bit different from that of the rest of us" (*Wall Street Journal*, 1978). The idea of a good society may not be widely shared. When Huckleberry Finn was lectured about heaven and found out what he would have to give up to get there, he said, "I made up my mind I wouldn't try for it." The good society and the real society are by definition at odds.

NOTES

1. Many of Dickens's heroes, like Oliver Twist, David Copperfield, and Pip in *Great Expectations,* find their way to the opportunities of bourgeois life. The ending of the penultimate chapter of *Great Expectations* summarizes with quiet satisfaction what Pip and his partner have accomplished: "We were not in a grand way of business, but we had a good name, and worked for our profits, and did very well" (Oxford University, 1970: 455-456).

2. Trilling's famous lines are from his essay on *The Princess Casamassima* in *The Liberal Imagination:* Essays on Literature and Society. He writes that from such novels dealing with the rise of outsiders, "we have learned most of what we know about modern society, about class and its strange rituals, about power and influence and about money, the hard fluent fact in which modern society has its being" (1950: 63).

3. Advertising books sometimes make the somewhat shamefaced admission that it is difficult to tell whether advertising works. One of the oldest chestnuts in the industry is the saying that 50% of advertising is effective — but no one knows which 50% it is. For recent discussions of advertising effectiveness, see Nelson (1974: 56-57; Nicosia, 1974b: 244-281).

4. See Leiss (1976: 89). Leiss states elsewhere that:

> The hidden dilemma for any society which attempts to sustain a high-intensity market setting is, simply stated, that even a steadily increasing array of commodities cannot alleviate the threat of scarcity as it affects the everyday lives of individuals. The dilemma is rooted in the fundamental characteristic of this setting, mainly, the tendency to orient all needs toward the realm of commodity consumption. . . . This kind of society is beset with a permanent contradiction between expanding wealth on the social level and intensified experiences of scarcity on the individual level [1976: 31-32].

In other words, a redefinition of Malthus is being attempted — not, I think, successfully.

2

ADVERTISING AND SOCIAL CONTROL

Like everything else transmitted by media, advertising says more than it states. Many of its critics believe that advertising is a form of "social control" — that is, of propaganda aimed at consumers. The following chapter considers the ways in which advertising may — or may not — use ideas to persuade us of much more than good reasons for consumption.

MEDIA AND MORES

In his monumental survey of *The Last Half-Century,* Morris Janowitz (1978: 320-363) describes the de facto function of mass media under industrialism as teaching standards of behavior to a large, disorganized public and suggesting alternatives to the problems of social life. Media — for the most part television, which occupies as much as 40% of the leisure time of our adult population — inform as much as they entertain. They may be said to provide "a flow of materials which fashion normative standards and which implant a picture of social reality" (Janowitz, 1978: 338). Advertising contributes to this function as well as programming. But, within both advertising and programming — within all media in general — there has been a great shift in the way that social ideas have been conveyed:

The idols in the mass media up until 1924 were men and women of economic, industrial, and technological achievement. They created goods and machinery. The change in emphasis came rapidly and decisively by the end of the 1920s. The development of an advanced industrialism, in the context of a consumer-oriented society, meant that the idols of consumption became more dominant and more central [Janowitz, 1978: 338].[1]

The concern with the management of interpersonal behavior means also that ordinary people become the idols and become more important. Progressively, the range of "encounters" has been broadened to include race relations, mental health, and familial arrangements [Janowitz, 1978: 339].

To accept the first passage means that we accept a profound dissociation. We know that the moral and fictional themes of the age of production, from Dickens to Hemingway, were sacrifice, heroism, and suffering. But, the themes of the age of consumption appear to be utility, satisfaction, and "the strategies human beings use to handle . . . personal and emotional problems" (Janowitz, 1978: 339). What are we to make of this change and diminution?

The passage ought certainly to be tested against fiction, nonfiction, and (something apart from both) television programming and commercials. It would seem to be partially true when applied to fiction. We do in fact seem to have passed from an age of *ethos* to one of *pathos*, from acting to being acted upon. And indeed many critics of modern fiction deplore its antiheroism and absence of moral interest. The "idols" portrayed by high culture seem to be less tragic than pitiable. In general, since the decline of Hemingway (which coincides roughly with the advent of consumption as a social style), the novel has been about victims (see Berman, 1968: 231-254). If there is such a thing as the typology of the American hero of achievement, then Charles Lindbergh found his complement in Jay Gatsby — and we have found ours in Woody Allen.

Granted that there are many exceptions, the passage seems to correlate with nonfiction — or with that part of it which articulates the values of therapy, self-help, and self-fulfillment. Within this realm, mental health is treated as if it were not only the principal end of existence but also as if it were a commodity generally available. One of the cant words of the movement is in fact "transaction," that is, a trade of anxieties for satisfactions.

The participant in therapy can be almost anyone, although few but the educated middle class have the interest or discretionary income that is necessary. One can "experience" drugs, psychodrama, encounter, or deep massage among the infinite alternatives of treatment. But the interesting thing from the point of view of consumption is that these are all in effect transactions. Mental health has no particular connection to action or belief. It is defined as a set of *attitudes* about the self and as *services* available to all.

Finally, this passage seems to be largely true when measured against programming and almost wholly true when measured against commercials. The world of television is a world of mass personal problems identical for everyone. Television presents the social life of the middle class; conveys its style, values, and situations; and suggests ways in which to carry on that life.

If moral problems have departed from the novel, they have been reborn for television. Both programming and advertising display the "big" problems of social life like race relations and the "little" problems like getting along with other people on the job. Programming and advertising are to some degree epideictic, displaying what are intended to be shared opinions. The show resolves a social problem while the commercial often solves a personal one. But there are some significant differences: As Janowitz puts it, programming has "shifted the locus of responsibility" from individual to social environment

(1978: 339).[2] Since we are franchised members of the Age of Consumption, we are less sinning than sinned against. Ours is to suffer the (temporary) inequities of life for 30 or 60 minutes and then to rationalize them. On commercials, however, we do not see ourselves as others see us, but in our own mind's eye. Commercials, as drama themselves, enact some of the few forms of bourgeois heroism that are left.

The programming may find some obsolete prejudice like Jim Crow conveniently localized in a neighborhood crank and within 30 minutes it brings sweetness and light to social differences. It assumes essentially that no one is guilty of anything but inadvertence. The commercial allows us to externalize certain feelings and to assert the values of the self against others who fail to recognize our efforts, talents, or even our beauty.

ADVERTISEMENTS AND SOCIAL STYLE

Commercials serve another role in the view of Daniel Bell, whose book *The Cultural Contradictions of Capitalism* is, like the Janowitz book, a landmark of social science. He observes that the Age of Consumption began in a society whose institutions of family, church, and education were naturally intent upon preservation and conservation of established values. This meant that new institutions had to cope with the value of change:

> A society in rapid change inevitably produces confusions about appropriate modes of behavior, taste, and dress. A socially mobile person has no ready guide for acquiring new knowledge on how to live "better" than before, and his guides become the movies, television, and advertising [Bell, 1976: 69].

The fact of social change has often stimulated new social institutions and created new kinds of media. In the late Renaissance, which was a time of the rapid ennoblement of wealth, a flood of handbooks on genteel behavior appeared. The aspiring elite were taught not only how to govern but also how to hold their knives and spoons. When Polonius tells his son Laertes in *Hamlet,* "Be thou familiar, but by no means vulgar," he is expressing the sententious tone of all such advice leading to upward social mobility. Be rich, he says, not gaudy. When the *Tatler* and *Spectator* give advice on manners and opinions in the Enlightenment, they serve the same social purpose.

Edmund Wilson's essay on Emily Post in *Classics and Commercials* reminds us of the same phenomenon in American life. The essay is about new kinds of authority for modern society. To Wilson's critical eye, Emily Post is not so much about etiquette as about social change. "Her book," he writes, "has some of the excitement of a novel. It has also the snob-appeal which is evidently an important factor in the success of a Marquand or a Galsworthy" (1950: 374). As he sees it, Emily Post's *Etiquette* has an understandable plot. At the top of the social pyramid are those who belong there through wealth or inheritance: the Worldlys of Great Estates and the Gildings of Golden Hall. Below them are a cast of social characters looking for a place in their Great Chain of Being — or in the sun. *Etiquette* is about the jockeying for position that takes place among those aspiring to social recognition, to a status befitting their desires. The book goes through the embarrassments of ruined dinners or late appointments or inappropriate dress to make a succession of cruelly logical conclusions: that manner, taste, and style are the new names for *carrières ouvertes aux talentes.* As Wilson says, Emily Post writes for post-Civil War society, in which social class, becoming more fluid, can only be asserted through consumption or display.

Mr. and Mrs. Unsuitable are dropped by society, and Mr. Vulgar, who crosses the Atlantic four times a year to associate with the smart set, succeeds only in making it plain to the Wellborns and Lovejoys how infinitely he is lacking the acquired graces. The Oldnames last forever; poor Miss Nobackground is repeatedly rebuffed. *Etiquette* is a primer of more than manners; it describes the interplay between inherited status and the power of money and style.

Since the advent of a popular press we have become used to validating change. Emily Post has written cruel even, in Edmund Wilson's phrase, sadistic little scenarios of the failure to match money with style. Amy Vanderbilt has told us which fork to use. Ann Landers now tells us the fine points of marriage, separation, and divorce. In short, media replace other institutions like school or church whose traditional function has been to guide everyday life. Daniel Bell writes,

> Advertising begins to play a more subtle role in changing habits than merely stimulating wants. The advertising in the women's magazines, the house-and-home periodicals, and sophisticated journals like the *New Yorker* was to teach people how to dress, furnish a home, buy the right wines — in short, the styles of life appropriate to the new statuses [1976: 69].

The changes that Bell identifies seem to be superficial, but they imply other and much deeper kinds of social transformation. Manners and taste depend upon the ways in which social authority is exerted within the family. They affect the ways in which money is spent outside it. They begin to define the subtle differences between children, adolescents, and young adults, even to the establishing of economic distinctions dividing them into separate markets.

Simply to take style as one example, manners and taste suggest a new relationship between appearance and achievement. In a social world that has become so much "other-directed," style matters increasingly more than substance. It is economically important, with whole industries defining group identity vis-à-vis things owned, used, or possessed. It is psychologically important in that the individual can become part of a group instantaneously by equipping himself with its ideas or symbols. Certain things — blue jeans, hi-fi sets, book bags — establish cultural identity on the spot.

ADVERTISEMENTS AND SOCIAL MYTHS

But the world of advertising is of course concerned with more than style, because to rely on style is to be exclusionary. The very definition of style implies limits. Televised commercials may portray certain very conventional kinds of styles, but they are essentially about necessities. We remind ourselves that the five biggest advertising budgets in the United States are spent for the most part on food and on soap, as indicated by the opening set of figures in *TV Guide Almanac*. The major effort of advertising is to communicate ideas about necessities.

In what way does this communication involve social control? A splendidly complex answer has been provided by a rather difficult book called *Hidden Myth*. The author, Varda Leymore, tries to get at the exact content of social control by a structuralist analysis of televised commercials. By combining this with anthropological interpretations, she has really provided us with a new tool for criticism. It is her contention that advertising has a central theme, the triumph of life over death. It is about consumption as a kind of primitive (but powerful) religion. Leymore has a memorable chapter on advertising vegetables which is frankly based upon the research of Lévi-Strauss on primitive tribes. Given the subject — a commercial on frozen potatoes and beans — the result is remarkable.

Leymore begins by describing the first frame, in which an old country woman is picking perfect vegetables and discarding all others. She of course no longer does so, because brand E has made that unnecessary: like the Fates, taking each vegetable off at its prime for the happy consumer. In other sequences, the product is conveyed by a homely delivery-wagon to a greengrocer, to be taken from there by the customer. By now there is an association between nature and brand E, between the idea of the seasonable and the product, between customer and an ancient and very satisfying idea of the personal marketplace.

Brand E comes "from brand E country," which is itself associated with home and mother. The old country woman is replaced by a smiling young housewife with children which are "like the perfect product, small, sweet and tender" (Leymore, 1975: 90). There are *no* men in this sequence. And, its "code" may be read as follows:

> Typical country scenes, endless fields, early morning sunrise, splendid isolation, silence and tranquillity, simple joys and quiet happiness, but above all else a close proximity to nature. The fields are never violated with modern brutal machinery. They are slowly and gently furrowed by an ancient primitive plough pulled by horses [Leymore, 1975: 91].

By a not very arcane symbology, spring, fertility, and pregnancy are associated with the product, which is set against winter, sleep, and death. The plough is both sexual and cosmic and linked by the horse pulling it to the old delivery-wagon of the first sequence. And the second sequence is full of ritual suggestions: wakening, warmth, sunlight, growing, even a kind of "typical Freudian imagery, a boy reclining over water rows a boat made of pod in a pond; and the pod, it is said, is filled with perfect little peas" (Leymore, 1975: 93).

The product itself is dead and frozen, but its language is mythologically about the continuation of life. It defies winter, ritualizes spring, suggests fertility against death, and presents woman in her likeness of Gaia, goddess of the earth. It is an archaic pantheon, composed only of the great mother, nature, and child-bearing — and a number of neatly frozen and packaged vegetables.

All this makes Dr. Dichter look pretty elementary, but it has its moments of conviction. There are archetypes for every kind of fiction, and evidently our latest genre is to that extent like every other. Where novels fail to discuss our collective unconscious, it may be presumed that commercials will take their place.

How arcane is the application of myth to advertising? In Dichter's (1975: 84) *Packaging: The Sixth Sense?* we find that consumers have a "Jungian collective memory" of home-made soap. In fact, the product is capable of sexual — certainly of sensual — arousal. It must be: a German detergent named Persil intended for the Spanish market was sufficiently "masculine" to carry the weight of a public relations campaign "in which the laundry detergent marries the linen" (Dichter, 1975: 93-94). The ingenuity of (or guilt for) imagination cannot be laid entirely at the feet of structuralism.

At any rate, Leymore concludes that advertising plays the same role in modern societies that myth does in primitive societies. She takes her categories from anthropology, essentially from the writings of Lévi-Strauss: in which myths exist to resolve social contradictions, to reinforce accepted behavior, and to conserve traditions. In her view, advertising is far from being a force for change. It necessarily supports the social order by reducing anxieties and providing simple solutions for eternal human dilemmas. Advertising solves life's four great problems: "one will belong rather than be excluded, one will have happiness rather than misery, good rather than evil, life rather than death" (Leymore, 1975: 156).[3] It sells the mundane, but invokes the fabulous.

VIOLENCE AND THE CRITICS

It may be that advertising and the programming that it supports are forces for social disruption as well as social control. That is at least the view of Janowitz, who remarks that there has been a perceptible *decline* in the contribution of mass media to social stability. One reason for this is that our media have encouraged political distrust and cynicism; the second, and possibly most important, reason is that the content of media exploits our sensibilities. Televised violence, for example, seems to do a great deal to weaken social personality, to offer the wrong kind of ideas and models about behavior, and to reflect a selective and brutalized set of ideas about life (Janowitz, 1978: 329).

We are tempted almost uncritically to agree with this judgment, or to disagree only with qualifications. But while the general soundness of the observation is taken for granted in so many dialogues, essays, criticisms, and even on so many television shows, it has proven to be difficult to make a case for its particulars. I should begin my own consideration of the subject with a *caveat:* At least for the moment I am less interested in proving or disproving any view than I am in examining methods commonly used for those purposes.

One of the great problems of informed discussion is the ideology of research. This is particularly clear when we address the two big issues of the day: sex and violence on television.

I am especially concerned with a group of influential essays from the *Journal of Communication* which have been cited or accepted by government, foundations, or other enterprises in research. These essays are illustrative of a kind of principle of excess in American intellectual life. They are essentially forms of advocacy.

One essay basic to the rest attempts to quantify by listing the social class of criminals on television shows (Gerbner et al., 1978). This seems to be based upon objective consideration. But it is the conclusion that one finds troublesome — that the reason for portraying criminals as members of the upper class, particularly rich businessmen, is the conspiratorial anxiety of the networks to crush the social aspirations of its audience. The general thesis is that television is *literally* a form of social control: that it propagandizes tirelessly on behalf of a male, capitalist ruling class. Its intention in portraying crimes of violence committed by this class is to frighten everyone else into submission:

> Fear is a universal emotion and easy to exploit. Symbolic violence may be the cheapest way to cultivate it effectively. . . . Ritualized displays of any violence (such as in crime and disaster news, as well as in mass-produced drama) may cultivate exaggerated assumptions about the extent of threat and danger in the world and lead to demands for protection. What is the net result? A heightened sense of risk and insecurity (different for groups of varying power) is more likely to increase acquiescence to and dependence upon established authority [Gerbner and Gross, 1976: 193-194].

The reader may wish to ask why fear rather than sex is a universal, and in what psychology it has been accepted as a prime source of motivation. He will wish to see clarified the "symbolic" nature of violence, especially since we already know from Aristotle's *Poetics* that ritualizing the violent events of tragedy by staging them is a form of purgation. He will certainly be curious about some hidden assumptions: that television is an arm of the state and that human nature is so easily influenced by fiction.

Even the definition of violence is arguable. If a character on stage gains emotionally by a social encounter, then he has "power" — if not, then he is a "victim." If leading characters are exclusively male, then programs offend decency by their replication of a social order which is inherently illegitimate. And an act of violence may be constituted by any kind of social activity: It may be violent for a male employer to give an order to a female subordinate or for a child to be told to mind his manners.

Within this group of surveys in the *Journal of Communication* it is observed that violence on screen is not a random but an intentional act of social aggression:

Middle-class characters "*do* the most killing. Lower class characters are most likely to be killed" (Gerbner et al., 1978: 189). Their "social existence" is being denied (Gerbner and Gross, 1976: 182). On television, most of the evil in society is concentrated "at the top of the power hierarchy," a point which makes us reach not for *Social Indicators* but for Ben Stein's (1980) interesting study of Hollywood ideas about American society, *The View From Sunset Boulevard.*

Stein concludes exactly the same thing that the *Journal of Communication* does: On television, the upper classes are responsible for most crimes of violence. But his interpretation is very different. He observes that a counter-culture of Hollywood writers has to all intents and purposes invented the screen fiction of upper class crime. It has given us this mythology for two main reasons: These writers must in their daily lives deal with the institutionalized dishonesty of the film world; and they are political liberals who wish to expose social injustice (see Stein, 1980: 15-28). As Stein points out, the businessmen they meet resemble those they write about. As a consequence, many movie and television scripts depict dishonest businessmen and rentier capitalists. But, there is an essential difference: While the behaviorists believe that television scripts reinforce the concentration of social power, it seems that the writers believe that they attack it.

One of the conclusions of this piece from the *Journal of Communication* is unarguable, that exposure to television creates a view of social reality. There will be some difficulty in agreeing with a second conclusion, that this social reality is characterized by distrust, danger, and feelings of alienation. The same is true of a third conclusion, which is that programming stimulates such things as a public "tendency to justify violence, to expect U.S. involvement in a new war, to want the U.S. to keep out of world affairs, and to take specific personal protective action" (Gerbner et al., 1978: 206).

There are several kinds of unscientific bias displayed. One is in the interpretation of what is perceived: If, after all, violence is symbolic, then anything at all which implies differences of role or authority (or perhaps even of opinion) between the sexes, races, and social classes can be "violent." There is another bias in the interpretation of what is intended. If writing a script which shows that crime does not pay is designed to reinforce the values of capitalism, then surely Aristotle was wasting his time when he defined poetic justice several millenia ago. There is finally the bias of what is defined. The above makes no distinction between violence and force. Indeed, the whole article attempts to shade that difference, to suggest that conventional morality proceeds by coercion alone. In so doing, it consciously violates a distinction as old as political science itself: that between legitimate force and illegal violence. There are, after all, *some* ways in which a family or a nation is entitled to defend — even to assert — its values.

In short, force is much the same as violence; war is a kind of enlarged synonym of our current social practices; isolationism and self-protection are on their faces reprehensible. We ought to keep in mind the connection of ideology to social science when we consider the affects of advertising on social change.

A certain amount of research on programming and advertising proceeds from dogma. The surveys that I have mentioned deal primarily with violence, and their assumptions — generally the same as their conclusions — are these:

(1) Television is a form of social propaganda which diffuses the views of a ruling class.

(2) Television is especially concerned to depict scenes of violence because they threaten the audience and ensure its subservience to those in the power structure who are really in charge of our social order.

(3) The short-run goal of television is to market goods while its long-run goal is to force the population to become willing employees and passive citizens.

Because of this, there should be a certain amount of skepticism about the claim that violence or other moral aspects of life can be schematized. Behaviorists rush in where philosophers fear to tread.

SEX AND THE CRITICS

There is much the same problem with the interpretation of sexuality. Like violence, it is too often assumed to be a *literal* form of social control. Some studies of sexuality in commercials and in programming are very useful: We are reminded by an article on "Sex-Role Messages in TV Commercials" that in one group of television ads recently studied, 88% of the voice-overs were done by men and 75% of domestic commodities were represented on screen by women (O'Donnell and O'Donnell, 1978). That is, if not "stereotyping," then it is something fairly close to it. But we are reminded by other articles that while such interest in roles may be a natural outcome of concern for human rights it is sometimes indistinguishable from censorship (see O'Kelly and Bloomquist, 1976). I am not using "censorship" in a metaphorical way. Certain kinds of research are clearly intent upon the imposition of sanctions for such offenses as "sex-role stereotyping." That this puts them in the position of blacks who object to the strangulation of Desdemona by Othello or Jews who object to the performance of *The Merchant of Venice* matters not a whit, at least to them. The sanctions are real enough, or would be: ranging from disapproval to public admonition to the intervention of government in the production of scripts.

Advertising seems to be exempted from some of the privileges normally accorded to, say, literature. As a second essay on minority rights puts the matter, "although television is often charged with purveying negative or stereotypical images of women . . . apologists for the media generally counter that it is changing — adding more female stars and females as occupiers of previously male-defined roles" (O'Kelly and Bloomquist, 1976: 179). The statement is interesting because of its substance, which indicates the relationship of media and social change, and because it describes the current practice of self-censorship in American life. It may be of even more interest because of its implications. Tactically, we find that only a very small percentage of news programming has involved women and non-whites — while there have of course been large, even disproportionate numbers of women depicted as housewives on commercials. What does this mean strategically? Unfortunately, it seems to mean that "a medium such as television is merely one link in a vast network of sexist and racist images, attitudes, and institutional structures" (O'Kelly and Bloomquist, 1976: 183). But, is not more caution advisable in moving from figures to conclusions? It may even be that such conclusions are *imposed* upon statistics; that from the beginning no other kind of conclusion might be expected. If anything, the study of sexuality is even more loaded than that of violence. It certainly seems to have a predisposition or controlling theory.

Sexuality on television is the subject of many a behavioristic article whose controlling theory comes from Marcuse and whose energies come from personal involvement in movements of liberation. If violence is interpreted as a threat communicated to the majority by the power elite, then sex is its accompanying bribe.

Sexual freedom is interpreted by this kind of research as a form of sexual repression. One article on "Commercial Liberation" finds that advertising absorbs or co-opts the passions of revolution: After the advent of feminism, women were depicted in quasi-military roles, triumphing over germs and dirt in their household battleground.

Whether the perception (which seems true enough) is matched by the conclusion is problematic: Such advertising is "a transparent play on the liberated woman as castrating bitch, brandishing her weapons" (Warren, 1978: 171).

The presumption is that advertising is determined to undermine the sexual revolution. It neutralizes feminism by depicting women with a new sense of assertion and aggressiveness, but still confined to a household environment. It represents the female body only in order to suggest that each part must be deodorized, sprayed, or depilated. It suggests that women are infantile and to some degree autoerotic or capable of finding satisfaction principally through the embrace of commodities. In short, advertising is an instrument of "power and repression" (Warren, 1978: 172).

Very little attention has been paid to the kind of maneuvering that has to be done by advertising and the programming it supports. The values of the audience are not those of the networks, although the latter continually groan with the exertion of proving some identity. Director, cast, and producer are often — usually — at loggerheads. Nowhere have the realities of performance been better put than in a quatrain from Yeats:

. . . My curse on plays
That have to be set up in fifty ways,
On the day's war with every knave and dolt,
Theatre business, management of men.

The accustomed strains of performance lead to many paradoxes. Sex and race, which are part of the new agenda for middle-class cultural politics, have their own demands. Insofar as they are dictated by constituency interests, a bitter conflict is necessarily involved between dramatic forms and social facts. That is implied by the colossal understatement of one essay from *Public Opinion Quarterly* on what we should usually call censorship: "Effective pressures brought to bear on television producers have largely eliminated stereotyped portrayals" (DeFleur, 1964: 71). What is meant is that television now depicts a minimum of black crime and a maximum of women in roles of authority.

Television is not only a marketplace but also a forum of constituencies. "Effective pressures" or censorship are yet another form of social control. But even such pressures must deal with the variables of American society. There is a very pointed discussion of sexual liberation in a recent issue of *TV Guide* devoted to *One Day at a Time*. The show was conceived by Norman Lear not only to attract marketplace and network attention but also to present what he called "hard-edged women's issues" in ways that would win the approval of feminism. *One Day at a Time* is about a divorced woman with two daughters who must find their way among the sexual snares and opportunities of modern life. While originally designed to trade in sexual liberation, the show has turned into a series of compromises. Sometimes it seems to argue for pleasure, maturity, independence, and sexual freedom; and other times, for restraint, tradition, and adherence to the ideals of bourgeois marriage. To that degree the show is socially schizophrenic. It has one foot in each camp: The older daughter is sexually experienced while the younger one is sexually innocent. Naturally enough, not all the customers are satisfied. The great silent majority is troubled by intercourse outside of marriage; the smaller audience of the liberated dislikes the show's trailing of convention. Criticism has not been avoided, but divided. While the National Organization for Women (NOW) finds that the sexuality of the two daughters, Barbara (played by Valerie Bertinelli) and Julie (played by Mackenzie Phillips), has been overemphasized, the cast itself has another point of view:

> By the time Barbara faced The Question, the producers went to the extraordinary lengths of polling students on

three university campuses as to whether she should give in. The results: strong support for keeping her chaste.

Now 20, Valerie Bertinelli wasn't surprised: "I know a lot of girls who feel that way about themselves." And Franklin, draping a motherly arm around Bertinelli's shoulder, observes: "There's a cry out in the country for Valerie's character to remain virginal — she's the one role model on TV about whom young women can say, 'Here's a beautiful girl and her choice is to wait until she's married' " [Westover, 1980: 28].

The audience, imagined by politicized critics to be wholly other-directed, has an enormous residue of traditional opinions, beliefs, and prejudices. It is one of the great incalculables, which is probably why determinism, rationalism, behaviorism — all of the movements which depend on a priori reasoning — prefer not to take it into consideration.

BEHAVING RIGHTLY

Most people agree that media inform us how to behave, but they agree with very little else. One man's (or woman's) role model is another's stereotype. It all seems to depend on what theory has been selected to contain the facts. But I think that the main points can be discerned: They have to do with attitudes conveyed by advertising about the essential public modes of style, morality, status, social constituency, and change itself.

Advertising, as Daniel Bell reminds us, does communicate the news about cultural style. It tells us not only how to dress but also how to organize our lives. The bonanza of cooking magazines, for example, from Gourmet to the latest Cuisinart production Pleasures of Cooking, defines a very substantial social group, those impelled by their status to find some objective correlative for it. Cookery is associated not only with the Gallic pleasures but with travel, with patronage of infinitely elaborate little stores selling kitchen engineering, and with other forms of high culture. It now means acquaintance with wine, art, and manners. When Ben Jonson wrote about these things in his famous poem celebrating hospitality, "To Penshurst," he called them "mysteries." He was probably right, since they depend on perceptions and intuitions and are conveyed by the informal process of tradition. The surest indication that these mysteries have become part of middle-class style is mass advertisement and sales.

It is on some interest that *la cuisine* has reappeared in a world of fast food, junk food, and convenience food. It may well be a reaction to all that, if not what Leymore has called an essential mythology of life. A case may be made for the latter: Jonson calls the good things that women bring to be eaten "an emblem of themselves." I tend to think of the new cookery as a real style because it demarcates the function, standards, and purchasing power of a visible social group. It is more than a way to spend money. The art of cuisine legitimizes functions that have been attacked by feminism, functions which are all that many women have or can hope for. I do not especially think that its practice displays the kind of "creativity" often praised by the amateur arts. *La cuisine* is real: One has, after all, to eat it after it has been inspired.

There is of course an enormous difference between fashion and style. Fashion is forever on the wing. Style is what fashion would like to become. In some cultures the transition has been made: *Haute couture* is a way of life familiar to the student of anthropology, complete even to its totems and taboos. In our own culture, totems and taboos are forever in the process of being defined. There is a particularly good passage by de Tocqueville about this:

> In proportion as castes disappear and the classes of society approximate, — as manners, customs, and laws vary, from the tumultuous intercourse of men, — as new facts arise, — as new truths are brought to light, — as

ancient opinions are dissipated, and others take their
place, — the image of an ideal but always fugitive perfection presents itself to the human mind [Heffner, 1956:
157].

The last clause is not a bad definition of style in America.
As de Tocqueville perceives, the ideal of "fugitive perfection" comes from the majority and is transmitted in a
number of traditional and often unconscious ways. After
taking the place of 19th-century institutions, advertising
has had to do some of the things which they would once
have done. It tells us what we must do in order to become
what we wish to be. That may mean telling us how to
consume our way into the bliss of satisfaction, but it may
also commend the restraints implied by de Tocqueville.
Style is a matter of taboos as well as of totems. Even
marketing implies exclusion when it deals with style.

I have mentioned several other modes of social control
and will be discussing them at greater length, but it is
appropriate to conclude this chapter with special attention
to one of them, social constituency. When Janowitz summarized the replacement of the idols of production by
those of consumption in *The Last Half-Century*, he observed that we now tend to focus very much on ourselves.
All media devote an enormous amount of their coverage
to the depiction of "interpersonal relations." Advertisements show us getting along with others and even with
ourselves. There are, however, other highly interesting
themes of consumption. Surely one of the great motifs of
modern life is membership in the kind of group that I have
called a constituency. There are more of these groups than
can easily be counted. Once again, American life has become divided among warring tribes. Movements for or
against environmentalism, abortion, nuclear energy,
planned parenthood — or the Snail Darter or the Tellico
River Dam — now exercise a larger power than those
separate issues might imply. Every ruling passion seems

now to have its party. Politicians have come to despair of "special interests" because it is so difficult to enforce party discipline against them — although their existence can in part be traced to the practice of government, which rewards any identifiable organization. One supposes that a society to overthrow Congress might well obtain federal funds for the purpose if it observed affirmative action and contributed to campaigns.

The fragmentation of the body politic into countless constituencies is one of the consequences of enlarged freedom. Identifiable public organization is personal character writ large. And in many respects it is very much to be valued. But, if Congress finds some difficulty in handling the matter, it is no wonder that advertising finds the same. It must not only accommodate the variousness of American life but also find the right role models — or even stereotypes — to take to market.

A modern de Tocqueville might now be struck both by the undifferentiated equality of American life and by the constitutencies into which it has broken itself up. It is richly divided into schools of politics or education or therapy or diet; into various kinds of assertions of rights; into organizations, associations, societies, auxiliaries, causes, and lobbies for the attainment of almost incredibly particularized ends.

Advertising is beginning to show the effect of this kind of cultural dialogue or monologue. It tends, with a certain uncertainty or nervousness, to emphasize the femininity of women: trying to cope with identity rather than with sexuality. It tries to capitalize on issues like environmentalism and the special problems caused by liberation: a father having to cook his own meals or a women in a difficult position of authority. All of this means a good deal more than the management of daily problems. It means that we tend to see ourselves in newsprint or on the television screen as dialectically involved in civic life, as adversaries or advocates. We are given clues to the nature of public issues and (sometimes) provided with answers to the questions they pose. More important, we are given clues to our own predicament: We see ourselves engaged in a wide-ranging cultural debate. It is not that advertising has suddenly become philosophical or that the middle class is now an intellectual estate: We are characteristically viewed by advertising, by media in general, as having political and cultural delineation. The consciousness of this kind of selfhood is important to any society; for our own it may be indispensable. Few other societies have had to create that sense of self in a world of Heraclitean change. For better and worse, we see ourselves becoming as well as being.

NOTES

1. It is noted here that the opposition of idols of production and those of consumption was originally theorized by Leo Lowenthal.

2. Janowitz notes elsewhere (p. 340) that on television at least, "in the popular presentation of the ironies of interracial marriage, divorced status, or unconventional sexual arrangements, there are no outcomes but a series of ongoing dilemmas." In short, no one on these programs is responsible for an ending or assertion.

3. Elsewhere Leymore discusses the role advertising plays in regard to the reconciliation of eternal opposites:

> The division of labour among the three parties — the original producer, the manufacturer and the final consumer — is complex. The original producer is allocated the constructive role of creation (life). The manufacturer is given the violent role of the killer and the processor (death). He is transforming the living thing — animal, bird, fruit or vegetable — into various forms of palatable death. And the consumer is given the thankless role of the carcass-eater, the one who has to feed on death in order to live. This impossible dilemma between the ferocious aspect and the human aspect of societal life, and, moreover, the absolute helplessness of man to solve this inherent contradiction, in which life can be nourished only through death, and in which man can only be either the killer or the vulture, is one of the basic conflicts of human life [1975: 97].

3

MARKETPLACE AND SOCIAL CHANGE

We often think of advertising as if it were a modern invention, but it is nearly as old as history itself. If we are to judge from literary and historical example, advertising has often shaped our imagination. At this particular historical moment, advertising defines middle-class expectations. It tells us not only the price of commodities, who produces them, and where they may be found but also why we ought to have those commodities, and what they will do for us. Most of all, advertising describes life in an industrial democracy. It never lets us forget that a mass market dominates all production — and it never ceases reminding us of what that mass market is like.

DESIRES IN DAILY LIFE

The critique of advertising that I have so far discussed is partly based upon conceptions of politics and of human nature. It tends to be Platonic rather than historical, preferring to determine the course of future social order rather than be guided by the probabilities of the past. That critique has many aspects and these should all be given their due weight: from the conviction of Marcuse that consumption is a form of sexual transference and repression to that of environmentalists who believe nothing more uncomplicated than that the use of scarce resources is unwise. It includes those who find advertising to be the voice of capitalism or of mass culture and of values un-characteristic of the emancipated mind, values which can rather easily be changed or extirpated. It does not include many who have simple, untheoretical, and legitimate ob-jections to salesmanship everywhere in their lives.

One of the repeated themes of theoretical criticism, for want of a better term, is the artificiality of desires: the conception more or less being that the law of diminishing returns can be repealed. I have suggested that social rationalism is utopian. It necessarily prefers to deal with the future because history is unsatisfying and intractable. While I find that most arguments attacking human frailty are worth the listening, I take with a grain of salt those that judge it by standards historically invisible. At present, a good deal of argument condemning advertising and productivity is based upon the insubstantial assumption that human desires are or should be rational. It tends not to consider the realities of material life or the reasons for social change.

The fact of advertising has been with us for millenia. Let us see how that fact can be interpreted. Simply as a datum, in Alexis Lichine's *Encyclopedia of Wines & Spirits* we find an account of a trade war in the first century A.D. involving the makers of rival products. When the Romans marketed their famous Falernian wine, it posed a com-mercial threat to the traditional vintages from the Greek islands of Chios, Lesbos, and Thasos. Keats (1899: 142) may have dreamed of Chian wine, with "beaded bubbles wink-ing at the brim, And purple-stained mouth," but the manu-facturers, more prosaically, were concerned with trademarks. Lichine (1973: 205) states that, knowing "the value of publicity," the Greek vintners retaliated by having "coinage stamped with clusters of grapes or with the head of Dionysos." It was something like putting Gallo Pinot Chardonnay on our own currency — right next to In God We Trust. The ruins of Pompeii, also from the first century, still show shop displays and signs to the weary traveller.

We are reminded by the indefatigable Chrétien De Troyes that the great Champagne Fair in medieval times was not only a thing of beauty but also that it corresponded to the idea of plenitude:

. . . the whole town
Filled with many fair people;
The moneychangers's tables covered with gold and silver
And with coins;
He sees the squares and the streets
Filled with good workmen
Plying their various trades:
One making helmets, one hauberks,
Another saddles, another shields,
Another bridles, and another spurs,
Still another furbishes swords,
Some full cloth, others dye it,
Others comb it, others shear it;
Others melt gold and silver,
Making rich and beautiful things [Gies and Gies, 1973: 76].

It is a social spectrum of the medieval world, which combines plenitude with order. Commerce is in its due place on the chain of being, with its displays indicating the use, abundance, and necessity of created things. The division of labor implies diversity as well as hierarchy. But there is of course a less emblematic side of things: Salesmanship in these stalls was so aggressive as to be a modified form of assault and battery. The moment even a single customer approached, tailors leaped off their stools and shoemakers jumped up from their benches, surrounding him and shouting the virtues of their product. Evidently medieval "advertising" had to be restrained by guild rules (Gies and Gies, 1973: 77).

One supposes that the history of advertising is in some respects also the history of regulation. Later, in the Renaissance, advertising came to be perceived as a correlative of hidden desires. There is a powerfully interesting scene in

Volpone in which Jonson's hero disguises himself as a mountebank or snake-oil peddler and addresses the hopes and fears of the Venetian crowd. Here is his prescription for their fears:

> . . . A most sovereign and approved remedy: the *mal caduco*, cramps, convulsions, paralyses, ill vapours of the spleen, stoppings of the liver, the stone, the strangury, *hernia ventosa, iliaca passio;* stops a *dysenteria* immediately; easeth the torsion of the small guts; and cures *melancholia hypocondriaca*, being taken and applied according to my printed receipt [Jonson, 1967: 81].[1]

Volpone even goes on to bemoan the imitations of competitors, to explain the cost of production, and to suggest the enormous amount of research needed to restore life, health, and sexual potency. How fictional is this? Not very. Frank Mott's standard history of *American Journalism* reprints from a colonial newspaper the claim of a panacea said to be excellent for "Weakness, Trembling of the Heart, want of Appetite, Gravel, Melancholy, and Jaundice" — as well as being a specific for colic, gout, and most kinds of fever.[2] The thought of its being actually used makes us hope that it was more harmless than effective.

There is an extremely important question about cultural style and consumption in Fernand Braudel's history of *Capitalism and Material Life 1400-1800:* "Is fashion in fact such a trifling thing? Or, as we think, do these signs constitute evidence in depth concerning the energies, possibilities, demands and *joie de vivre* of a given society, economy and civilisation?" (1973: 235). Braudel is one of the leading historians working today, and he has revitalized historical inquiry with this question. Part of the answer to it lies in style, literature, consumption, and daily experience insofar as it has been recorded or can be deduced. If we go back to Jonson's *Volpone* we can see to what extent it provides "evidence in depth" of human experience. The play has two songs deserving to be famous, although only one of them, "To Celia," has caught the attention of literary history. The other may be equally compelling. It is sung by Volpone to the Venetian crowd as he divines their need for his prescription. The first passage I quoted from *Volpone* was about human fears; this one is about human hopes:

You that would last long, list to my song,
Make no more coil, but buy of this oil.
Would you be ever fair? and young?
Stout of teeth? and strong of tongue?
Tart of palate? quick of ear?
Sharp of sight? of nostril clear?
Moist of hand? and light of foot?
Or I will come nearer to't,
Would you live free from all diseases?
Do the act your mistress pleases,
Yet fright all aches from your bones?
Here's a med'cine for the nones [Jonson, 1967: 85-86].

This song ought certainly to be read against "To Celia," which is about love made fleeting by the passage of time. But its terrible urgency, its desire to "live free," might be read against another and even more famous passage from Shakespeare which distills Renaissance pessimism about the end of our strange eventful history in,

. . . second childishness and mere oblivion,
Sans teeth, sans eyes, sans taste, sans everything.[3]

Fashion, style, and consumption seem to be part of what Braudel calls "evidence in depth." They may not constitute the kind of evidence we should like, but about that Braudel has something to say:

If luxury is not a good way of supporting or promoting an economy, it is a means of holding, of fascinating a society. *Civilisations – strange collections of commodities,*

*symbols, illusions, phantasms and intellectual models –
work in this way.* An order becomes established that
operates down to the very depths of material life [1973:
243; emphasis added].

And, in fact, the kind of history that Braudel writes, the
kind of history which has over the last decade become
dominant, is about what he calls the "realities" of life:
food, drink, housing, clothes, and fashion. It matters very
much that consumption should be unnecessary, vulgar,
and luxurious, and that advertising should reflect that. It
matters even more that history is no longer being written
about politics and diplomacy as if they were the only
"realities."

CONSUMPTION: THE GREAT REALITY

The burden of the new history, whether applied to the
growth of capitalism in France or to the condition of slaves
in America, is the importance of daily experience. The new
quantitative history not only depends expectably on re-
cords but it also tries to estimate the general material
circumstances of life for the mass of men. As Braudel, who
is its most famous practitioner, writes, the new history
must be as conscious of style as of treaties and diplomacy.
It takes consumption seriously because that has been an
important measure of participation in society. That has not
been unnoticed by art, from Trimalchio's Feast, which
expresses the decadence of first-century Rome, to Sancho
Panza's daily onion and dried bread, which corresponds to
the simplicity of his expectations.

Consumption has been a major Western mode since
the High Middle Ages. The reasons for preindustrial consumption are roughly the same as those for postindustrial
consumption: a relief from the bitterness and tedium of
labor; an aspect of urban life created by medievalism; a
ceremonial flouting of death as Volpone shows it in a

world of poverty, disease, and heartbreakingly low life expectations; and the symbol as well as actuality of social change. There have been new reasons added in modern times, but the old ones have not been displaced.

In asking us to modify or reform consumption, critics of productivity are asking no more than was asked by the medieval church which was deeply conscious of the relationship of charity to poverty. But reform now may have as difficult a time now as it did then. Medieval history is full of reminders that purchase, display, and consumption were desperately sought by the mass of men.[4] But consumption triumphed over morality and sumptuary laws and satire — over everything but scarcity. Our own idea of plenitude right now tends to be emotional — that is, I think, an accurate way of referring to the regnant ethic of self-realization. We are unsparing in our praise of those mechanisms or experiences that contribute to *psychological* satisfaction. And we believe there is no end to them, nor ought to be. But "fulfillment" is a form of consumption in a time untrammelled by scarcity. The preindustrial world lived in scarcity and its dream, expressed by Chaucer in *The Canterbury Tales*, was of the Franklin in whose house, "It snowed . . . of meat and drinke."

Renaissance history indicates that the aesthetics and psychology of consumption were central to civic life. Here is what Plumb has to say about the materiality of art:

> They pursued physical beauty like a drug. Their heightened sensibilities, due to the sudden turns of chance which threaded their days with light and shadow, lusted for color, richness, wanton display. This aristocratic spirit at large in a world of bourgeois delights had no use for pewter dishes, sober costume, modest feasting, or chaste jewelry. It reveled in gold, in silver, in bronze, in gaudy dishes of majolica, and in silks, in satins, and in damasks, in cunningly wrought pearls, in sapphires, in rubies, and in emeralds [1965: 43].

The impression one gets of the Renaissance from textbooks is that it consisted for the most part of large ideas. The impression one gets from museums is very different: As Plumb puts it, the Renaissance was a festival of excess. But his description of it seems altogether too sober and restrained when compared to the dream of Sir Epicure Mammon in Jonson's *Alchemist:*

> My meat shall all come in, in Indian shells,
> Dishes of agat set in gold, and studded
> With emeralds, sapphires, hyacinths, and rubies.
> The tongues of carps, dormice, and camels' heels,
> Boiled in the spirit of sol, and dissolved pearl,
> Aspicius' diet, 'gainst the epilepsy:
> And I will eat these broths with spoons of amber,
> Headed with diamond and carbuncle [1963: 240].

This is polymorphous perversity on a scale of magnitude undreamed of by Norman O. Brown or Herbert Marcuse. It is also pretty clearly a manifestation of human nature under Western conditions of life.

Victorian literary history reminds us what a festival of consumption the art of Dickens celebrated. He wrote about dark cities and satanic factories as impediments to the good bourgeois life. The stories of Mr. Pickwick and Tiny Tim belong with those of Falstaff and Sancho Panza: If tragedy is a matter of sex, comedy appears to be a matter of eating and drinking. Reform ought to be advised, as *Measure for Measure* tells us, that lust will never disappear "till eating and drinking be put down." One supposes that human nature remains the same and that difficulties arise when conditions change. Desire awaits excess. Either that or we have read Blake for nothing.

Behind the undisputed excesses of productivity and consumption are several millenia of group experience. We all want more, although it remained for Samuel Gompers to make that an expression of policy. Of course, he was not the first to do so, having been anticipated by Oliver Twist. And we all want through the mode of consumption to keep death at a distance. In the last chapter I mentioned Varda Leymore's adaptation of Lévi-Strauss, in which advertising becomes a way of visualizing the passage from eating dead carcasses to sustaining our own lives. There is no question in my mind that consumption, as a ritual, keeps away death. Surely that is plainly implied by Jonson, by Shakespeare, by Browning's Bishop ordering his tomb at Saint Praxed's, and by all those other poets who have dealt with material desires.

Most men have no other way to measure social change than by getting more. Some, like Alexander Pope's bourgeois merchant, can only conceive of more of the same. Enriched by shipwreck, he assumes a new, inflated social style — "And lo! two puddings smoked upon the board." The issue of whether getting more is good or bad is right now a burning issue, but it may be academic. Argument cannot affect the fact that the mass has been brought into Western society by the changing conditions of material life. Emancipation has taken place in the form of more income, expenditure, and opportunity. There is another fact, that we interpret improvement as consumption. In short, what we call "culture" extols commodities as well as symbols and ideas.

The leisured class, as described by T. S. Eliot in terms even more pointed than those of Veblen, has measured out its life in coffee spoons. The working classes have measured out their lives by the equities of industrialism, that is, by their share in what Braudel has called the "realities."

We often ascribe advertising to the modern fact of underconsumption.[5] The general argument is that industrialism made advertising necessary in order to adjust demand upward toward supply. In some respects this is true, but it leaves out the earlier history of advertising. I have mentioned Volpone in the Venetian marketplace and the lessons drawn by Jonson for his own audience. The heart of the matter was the sale of life and health to a society in which these particular goods were in short supply. The poetry of *Volpone* is about what Plumb has called heightened sensibilities in the face of death. Whether we take Jonson's salesman in *Volpone* or Shakespeare's peddler Autolycus in *The Winter's Tale* we can see that although what they sell is valueless, the purpose for which it is sold is eternal. The same can be said of later times.

IN SICKNESS AND IN HEALTH

That would certainly seem to be the case in dealing with an identical situation three centuries later and in another country. *The Physician and Sexuality in Victorian America*, a superb study of sickness, treatment, and nostrums, tells us in great detail the relationship of advertising to natural human desires. Long before there was public "underconsumption" a characteristic relationship obtained between certain products and certain needs. The snake-oil salesman of the 19th century resembled his counterpart of the 17th century: Both sold what was essentially an existential idea. It was meant, as certain ideas about commodities are always intended to mean, to keep death at a distance.

Nineteenth-century life is close to us but it was in some respects closer to medieval life. It was agrarian, subject to the same limits and diseases as all life before the era of immunization. It was a life of high mortality. There were times when that mortality, particularly at childbirth, reached 100%. Those who made it to adulthood could look forward to essentially medieval dentistry and surgery. The eternal human desire to "live free" was confronted by rather high odds against it. Medicine became patent medicine because that desire was too strong to be contained by certainty.

As we look over the old advertisements of the 19th century we are struck by their resemblance to magic. The market for Brown's Iron Bitters was assured that the product was a certain cure for diseases requiring a complete tonic, indigestion, dyspepsia, intermittent fevers, want of appetite, loss of strength, lack of energy, malaria and malarial fevers, etc. Removes all symptoms of decay in liver, kidneys and bowels, assisting to healthy action all functions of these great organs of life. Enriches the blood, strengthens the muscles and gives new life to the nerves [Haller and Haller, 1977: 297].

The vocabulary has changed very little in 300 years: Like Volpone's magic potion, this is directed at specific threats to life — *and to ideas about health*. Ben Jonson is a better copywriter, but both he and the anonymous creator of claims for Brown's Iron Bitters sense something about human desires. Even when something *isn't* specifically wrong we want vitality, beauty, appetite, and sexuality.

That is one of the keynotes of advertising both before and after industrialism. As one advertisement for Dr. Scott's Electric Flesh Brush puts it, the commodity really being sold is "New Energy and New Life" (Haller and Haller, 1977: 155).

It makes us reflect not so much on the claims of advertising but on the conditions of life for the mass of men and women. There were two great questions: how to live "free" of the painful and often disgusting adjudications of Nature and how to choose between their cures? As *The Physician and Sexuality* states, "from Vaughn's Vegetable Lithontriptic to Morison's Vegetable Medicine to Dr. Ward's Unfortunate Friend, the claims covered everything from split toenails to syphilis, bilious fever, and insanity" (Haller and Haller, 1977: 265).

The mercury treatment for syphilis and various opiates for neurasthenia were routine, if fumbling attempts to cope with social habits. The mercury treatment, advertised variously as a "life balsam" or "blood purifier," resulted in serious deformities and ulcerations. It may well have been more effective, however, than sulfur fumigations, sarsaparilla, or spirits of lavender. As for opiates, those who drank Lydia Pinkham's Vegetable Compound were often unaware that it was 40 proof, which may not have been so bad: Hoofland's German Tonic was 60 proof and Boker's Stomach Bitters, at 85 proof, was about the level of blended bourbon. The amount of chloral, bromide of sodium, opium, and morphine consumed by women was staggering. These "tonics" were intended to make life more bearable, but one could become an addict at the soda fountain (Haller and Haller, 1977: 281-289).[6]

In short, insofar as the ability to carry on social life could be symbolized by a commodity, many men and women risked death for it.

Advertising was involved in the sale of these poisons, as were many druggists and physicians. The level of scientific information in 19th-century medicine was fairly low. These highly advertised nostrums and panaceas were related to what the medical historian has called the peculiar difficulties of the age: its universal silence about sexual vice and its universal praise of unreachable virtue. Commodities like Nervura and Peruna, capable of disposing of whole laboratories of mice and a wilderness of monkeys, were readily dispensed to housewives by their neighbors. They were perceived as modes of social rationalization: keeping women from nervous collapse and keeping men with their noses to the grindstone. Vice was everywhere, but was everywhere unspoken: Its unnerving presence in the human heart needed a tonic now and then. As for virtue, that may have been harder to cope with. These commodities were sold on the basis of their contribution to a normal life and its values, without the interruptions of depression or ill-health. Half a century before the publication of Huxley's *Brave New World*, middle-class society was opiated into a model of its ideal.

With this in mind, one wonders at the liberating effect of consumption. But there was such an effect, and it involved more than the substitution of marijuana for Peruna. Consumption in modern times has become a way of making dreams real. Before modern times those "realities" described by Brandel were, at least for the masses, pitifully inadequate.

In premodern times the eternal desires for life, health, comfort, well-being, and beauty had limited correlatives. The marketplace could not fulfill such desires. Most people, even as late as the turn of the century, resigned themselves to the facts of life in an economy of scarcity. Chief among these in the United States was a life expectancy of about 47 for whites *and about 33 for blacks* (U.S. Department of Commerce, 1977: 190-191). There were few commodities which, like penicillin, might bring comfort, affect health, or extend life. Under industrialism such commodities did reach the marketplace. Claims that sounded insane when made for Balm of Gilead or Paine's Celery Compound — or for Volpone's elixir of life — were the simple actualities of the new pharmacopoeia. The desire for health and life, hitherto associated with magic or fantasy, now became fulfilled by actual products like soap. The effect lingers on; altogether too much advertising continues to use the idiom of magic to suggest the affect of commodities on life. But in some respects, especially when comparing current life and its standards to the recent past, science must seem like a form of magic.

History has a way of translating necessities. What begins as a utopian vision of the future often ends as an accepted fact. After the demands of millenia had been met by goods which actually did result in longer and better lives, there were a number of social redefinitions. What had before been luxuries (for example, indoor plumbing and refrigeration) translated themselves into necessities. In general, we dislike this process unless we benefit from it directly. Since the conversion of luxuries into necessities inherently involves the distribution of *styles* as well as of goods, it means that social classes become aware of their opposition. It becomes easy to attack the masses because of their ridiculous emphasis on things that the elite is ready to discard. Or, it becomes possible to attack them, as Dickens suggests in his brilliant novel of industrialism, *Hard Times,* for aspiring to the same conditions of life as their betters. Bounderby the industrialist is convinced throughout *Hard Times* that what the factory hands really want is "turtle soup" rather than 10-hour days.[7]

The Census Bureau, which keeps figures on automobiles, television sets, clothes washers, freezers, dishwashers, and air-conditioners, indicates that these are owned by a majority of Americans. The review of these statistics in Ben Wattenberg's *The Real America* and in *Social Mobility in Industrial Society* by Seymour Martin Lipset and Reinhard Bendix concludes that more is involved than material consumption. Wattenberg's book, although sometimes a panegyric to progress, does establish the relationship between commodities and social classes. His thesis is that the consumption or use of the appliances noted above has completely transformed the middle class. Owning the same things allows people to live the same way (Wattenberg, 1976: 103). The new middle class is infinitely larger than before industrialism. It has many more opportunities to improve or extend life. And, its arrival can be measured by the labor-saving commodities that it owns.

Lipset and Bendix write of something even more interesting:

> The *distribution* of consumers' goods has tended to become more equitable as the size of national income has increased. This relationship between wealth and the distribution of consumer goods has been commented on by the Swedish economist Gunnar Myrdal who writes, "It is, indeed, a regular occurrence endowed almost with the dignity of an economic law that the poorer the country, the greater the difference between poor and rich [1967: 108].

The United States, which is the richest of all countries, has also the most level distribution curve.

The question is how do we define the idea of progress? Is it the same for the mass as for the elite? Is progress a matter of ideas or is it a matter of actualities? The desire for survival has become, for the United States, replaced by that of betterment. Under current conditions, with longevity approaching the biblical threescore and 10, there has been a relaxation of existential fears. To be sure, they have been replaced by others. There is a wry passage in *The Cherry Orchard* in which Gayev remarks on another condition of 19th-century life: "if a great many remedies are suggested for a disease, it means that the disease is incurable." Chekhov of course was a physician, who knew for some time that he was going to die, quite young, of one of these diseases. The opposite condition prevails now with the habitual use of specifics that have replaced panaceas. With health as well as life now available in the form of commodities, the mass has been free to turn its attention to the real business of life, getting as much as possible.

Betterment has clearly taken the place of survival as a social issue. It is now widely assumed that Americans have a right to long life and good health: Their next agenda is participation in society and equality. As both Lipset and Myrdal have observed, equality is measured literally by the distribution of goods and services. It would be spendid if betterment were to be visualized in terms of altruism, but for the present it seems to be thought of in terms of income, possessions, and opportunities.

We know that betterment is morally insufficient. Yet the fact remains that the citizen of an industrialized country thinks of his life — of social life in general — as a matter of hours worked, income realized, and benefits gained. The idea of progress is for most people literal. Consumption has then become identified with liberation in these material, if limited ways. They do not include everything important to civilization and may in fact be said to exclude a great deal that is. But they indicate the contours of experience for the majority.

INVENTING THE CONSUMER

Advertising has been with us in its modern shape for about a century: as the voice of industrial enterprise on a national scale. In its first 50 years, as Daniel Boorstin (1973: 109-116) explains in *The Americans: The Democratic Experience*, changes occurred in structure as well as style. Department stores, with widely advertised wares and prices and with uniform commodities, began to replace the single-purpose store. The Sears, Roebuck catalogue replaced the old kind of salesman. There were obviously tremendous advantages for both merchant and customer in the new order of things but there were disadvantages as well. Their relationship became an abstraction. Old ideas could not be retained in new circumstances.

Boorstin uses the phrase "consumption communities" to suggest how much tradition had been affected. The country became citified as farmers all over the United States learned how to use mail-order catalogues. The cities became enormously enlarged versions of their medieval past, with the annual "fair" or market operating each day of the year.

Advertising, "destined to be the omnipresent, most characteristic, and most remunerative form of American literature," articulated these changes (Boorstin, 1973: 137). Its own format became symbolic. The famous "agate rule" which had governed typesetting since Colonial times was broken shortly before the Civil War. The tiny, really indistinguishable print gave way to a riot of design and illustration. Brand names became familiar and consumer loyalties were attached to them. As Frank Mott (1966: 594) states in his history of *American Journalism*, Aunt Jemima and Sunny Jim became folk heroes of a new art. Slogans like "Uneeda Biscuit" became part of our social imagination.

Other things became part of that imagination as well: (1) the recognition that advertising, particularly of patent medicines, could be dangerously misleading and (2) the movement (which included advertisers and newspaper publishers) to regulate the purity of food and drugs. The legislation of reform in marketing contributed to the general understanding that national life was a matter of goods and services.

Within that national life the most important social change was the invention of the consumer. After World War I the consumer became the economic equivalent of the "citizen" and his realm, created by advertising, was the marketplace.

Since that time, in our end of the 20th century, there have been three great kinds of change within that marketplace. The first has been in buying, selling, and credit. The new institutions of economic life — department stores, mail-order business, and an incredibly expanded banking system — could not begin to function without new modes of earning and payment. Credit, first used to sustain these institutions, had a subsidiary effect probably larger than its primary one. It became an economic form of equality, allowing those with different status but the same income to live in the same way. The second change concerns what we sometimes call "mass culture." Unlike more stratified societies, America does not take — no longer takes — the graphic form of a social pyramid. The "lower" classes are to a large extent the "middle" classes. Their earnings rival those of technical, white-collar, or other occupations relying on mental rather than manual labor. While physicians, lawyers, and executives make a great deal more money than anyone else, others regularly employed lead lives that have become indistinguishable. The skilled trades especially rival occupations with traditionally higher status: According to *Time* of June 9, 1980, a boiler technician earns almost $23,000 per year — which is higher than the average for tenured associate professors. Lipset and Bendix conclude in *Social Mobility in Industrial Society* that the universalized ability to buy commodities like a house or car is a form of equality that puts a new interpretation upon social status. It reconciles class differences, softens political conflict, and gives a literal measurement for social equity (Lipset and Bendix, 1967: 109-110). The third change has involved the communication of ideas — or nonideas. Advertising is but one of the effects loosed upon Western society by the power of literacy. Within the very recent past, literacy has become a commodity like any other. Its association with art and style has been broken. It is no longer a distinction of education; perhaps almost the opposite might be said. Literacy has undergone the utilitarian fate foreseen by de Tocqueville for all commodities in a democracy: the general aim of production being the lowest common denominator. That literacy should be regressive was unsurprising to Orwell or to those other writers over the past century who have charted its decline. The cultural observations of Matthew Arnold, Henry Adams, Van Wyck Brooks, Ezra Pound, T. S. Eliot, and Lionel Trilling have been largely devoted to the fate of excellence in a democracy (see Trilling, 1972; Eliot, 1950: 452-460).[8]

There are differences and sometimes compensations to be weighed against our losses. The vulgarity of media is balanced by their equality. Advertising's modern half-century coincides almost exactly with the development of the new middle class. Most of those in it are recent arrivals. It is made up of immigrants, minorities, and recycled older groups of citizens. It does not correspond to the middle class of 1930 and one of the best ways to comprehend this is to look at images of society displayed by literature, painting, and their imitations. For example, one of the great themes of F. Scott Fitzgerald's stories is the barrier of social class. In *The Great Gatsby* love turns out to mean less than money, style, and tradition. In *The Sun Also Rises* the distance between the aristocratic Brett Ashley and her incurably bourgeois admirer Robert Cohn is unfathomable. But, since the 1920s, the theme of literature and its mass culture imitations has been social mobility. The Snopses of Faulkner's *Hamlet* are a new class on their way up. Marquand's Willis Wayde and O'Hara's Julian English are the last, attenuated forms of the young man from the provinces, middle-class careerists.

Advertisements of the 1920s and 1930s seem now to be about another country. Everyone is not only white but desperately respectable. Men wear ties while playing golf and women dress informally as if for the membership committee of some particularly cranky country club. These old posters evoke a society under self-restraint: in which Coca-Cola is a reward of the Protestant Ethic. In these illustrations, phonographs play their Appollonian strains to a cast that went to Princeton. The subdued watercolor tints suggest unspoken boundaries of good taste. Copy is grammatically decorous, morally reassuring. Women are as stylized as their automobiles, drawn with a line as sharp as Picasso and in a way as abstract. There is no sexuality in these illustrations, only a perception of sex in terms of social class. It is a perfect inversion of Marcuse.

One of the ways to see a context for Fitzgerald is to look at advertisements of the 1920s. They show us the golden chariot of Daisy Buchanan and the sharply etched, distant cult figure of success whom she represents. They may even tell us something about the shirts in stripes and scrolls and plaids in coral and apple-green and lavender and faint orange that made her cry. They will certainly tell us how she thought:

"Ah," she cried, "you look so cool."
Their eyes met, and they stared together at each other, alone in space. With an effort she glanced down at the table.
"You always look so cool," she repeated. She had told him that she loved him. . . .
"You resemble the advertisement of the man," she went on innocently. "You know the advertisement of the man" [Fitzgerald, 1953: 78-79].

They are overheard by her husband, and by several million consumers.

A NEW MIDDLE CLASS

The Great Gatsby is about a special few; it was only after World War II that mobility became a fact for the majority. Until then, most people had closed expectations about their lives. Industrial romance, in the shape of soap operas and ladies' magazines, invoked dreams of all those things unlikely ever to happen: radical change in career, income, status, or personality. Until World War II the barriers to social class were as they had been described throughout American literature. Education, the exit from ascribed status, was not open to many.

In virtually no respect has middle-class life remained the same. Its old landmarks were small towns punctuated by vertical cities: Its new ones are suburbs and shopping malls. One of the best evocations of this change is in Theodore White's *In Search of History,* which is about living through the decades of social change. For White, the 1950s were a truly revolutionary age. They witnessed the translation of the energies of war into merchandising. They experienced prosperity on a scale never yet known. And, they were the age of television.

White's most perceptive comments on social change have to do with the shaping power of televised advertising. He worked for *Collier's,* which, like *Life, Look,* and *The Saturday Evening Post,* was to become a casualty of progress. Like these others, it failed to get enough advertising to continue. But it could see the reason why — the advertising salesmen knew that *Collier's* could not reach the new middle-class audience:

> I learned from them that thirty years earlier toothpaste was something heavily advertised in upper-class

magazines because poor people, non-readers, generally used no toothpaste at all; and now, "every workingman son of a bitch and his wife brush their teeth in the morning." So toothpaste-makers now relied on television and the supermarket to move toothpaste because "both the doctor's wife and the plumber's wife get their Wheaties at the same place" [1978: 428].

The tactical point is that television made magazines obsolete because it reached those who still did not read. The strategic point is that it fed the social politics of expansion. It was tuned to the newly discovered purchasing power of the masses, and necessarily to their expectations.

In its infancy, television brought us Groucho Marx, Sid Caesar, and Lucille Ball, which is an accomplishment. It also brought us wrestling "exhibitions," quiz shows, and *This Is Your Life*. The Emmy Award for Most Outstanding Personality of 1948 was given to Shirley Dinsdale and her puppet Judy Splinters, by no means an unrepresentative choice. Variety shows began their interesting career of reflecting mass culture, that is to say culture produced by those with education for those without it. But as television grew it became more obviously epideictic. Commercials as well as programming were made into little dramas of social life. The agenda of television was the presentation to itself of a large and relatively new social class. The family situation comedy became a vehicle of social consciousness, reminding us in the 1950s of adolescence as a national peculiarity, then in the 1960s and 1970s of racial identity, and now, in the 1980s, of sexual liberation. The family became a universal theme. In literature before television family life had often been tragic. The patriarchs of O'Neill's *Desire Under the Elms*, Faulkner's *Absalom, Absalom*, and Steinbeck's *To a God Unknown* were modern incarnations of Chronos the destroyer and creator. They were figures of primal-horde Freudianism, to be replaced in our cultural imagination by the cowards of the Age of Anxiety.

Televised comedy became a form of socialization. It depicted (and assisted) the loss of parental authority. As we look over the invaluable pages of *TV Guide Almanac* we can see to what extent the idea of social life has changed. From 1949 to 1980 the family situation comedy has provided images, ideas, and even guidelines for the relationships of husband and wife, father and son, lover and friend. It has revolved around the institutions of school, household, and job. I thas featured every conceivable "problem" of "interaction" — and in solving them, however falsely, has given us what Fitzgerald once wrote was a Platonic idea of ourselves. Each year, if we go by the ratings, there has been a typified American household: in 1949 it was the *Life of Riley;* in 1953 *I Love Lucy;* in 1961 the *Dick Van Dyke Show;* in 1966 *The Andy Griffith Show;* in 1972 *The Odd Couple;* in 1980, unfortunately for viewers, critics, and Western culture, *Laverne and Shirley.* With each passing year there have been structural changes keyed to larger events. The bourgeois family with three young children and a servant has been replaced by increasingly odd couples. The new "household" connections are between Mindy and Mork, Laverne and Shirley, and even Charlie's Angels. *The Mary Tyler Moore Show,* one of the first to take seriously the idea of a fragmented household, has given rise to bachelor singles, gay couples, platonic trios, and mixed doubles. Eventually, even eight may not be enough.

LEISURE FOR THE MAJORITY

The consequences have been fascinating, but of that more later. What matters here is a different kind of social message. If television is inseparable from mass culture, it is equally inseparable from mass leisure. The washing-machine that it sells, for example, is probably as revolutionary as Ben Wattenberg has suggested in *The Real America*. It is a precondition for the employment of women. The clothes washer and dryer have meant as much for women as the automobile did for men. They substituted for the hired help that was no longer available. They gave the bourgeois family that power over time and circumstance which defines a ruling class. The washer is generically important: the class of goods it represents began by making work easier and ended by changing human aspirations.

At one time there was a consensus, including artists and intellectuals, about these commodities. The movement we call Modernism began with what was quite literally a celebration of the machine. Hugh Kenner's book on 20th-century American writers, *A Homemade World*, suggests that the invention of the airplane was as much a triumph of and for Modernism as the writing of *Ulysses*. He begins discussion of Joyce, Pound, and Fitzgerald with a description of the Wright brothers achieving on the North Carolina shore a deed as great as the discovery of Troy (Kenner, 1975: xii). And Lionel Trilling (1973: 129), like Kenner aware that Daedalus symbolized both the machine and the mind, returns to the birth of Modernism in order to explain the relationship of our technology to our art. It was, he says, "the beauty and vitality of the machine" which provided the central theme of Modernism's great document, the Futurist Manifesto.

One machine in particular captured the imagination of modern artists and writers. Trilling says of F. T. Marinetti, the author of the Futurist Manifesto, that he "may have celebrated the machine in general but it is specifically the automobile that engages the enthusiasm" of his work. At least in the first decades of the 20th century this is the machine through which the individual expressed his will — which makes him, as Freud wonderingly stated, a kind of artificial God.

Literature was true both to life and to the manifesto. The automobile is at the heart of *The Great Gatsby*. Even as late as *The Reivers* of Faulkner it provides a theme of revolutionary change and freedom. But, since then the ways have parted, as we can see in the last few words of Robert Lowell's "For the Union Dead":

. . . Everywhere,
giant finned cars nose forward like fish;
a savage servility
slides by on grease.

These are wonderful lines, in part because both clauses are true. By the end of Modernism the machine took on a new thematic power. The automobile, which took Daisy Buchanan to Gatsby's castle by the sound, which roared through the back roads of Frenchman's Landing and carved up the Sutpen Hundred, and which brought Sweeney to Mrs. Porter in the spring had become demonic, at least for intellectuals.

There are now two disputed histories of social technology. One is based on the great mythical event of the 20th century, the revolt of the masses. In this version the automobile is a kind of Frankenstein's monster. It imposes upon society the standards of the philistines who own banks and stores and used-car lots from Oakland to Mineola. It pollutes the landscape and crowds the highways. Its style is a more or less continuous affront. In this version of history the automobile exemplifies the spirit of General Motors, not the linkage of man and machine so fleetingly admired in Lindbergh and the *Spirit of St. Louis*.

The other version is equally compelling. It is about large, powerful cars bought because energy was cheap, distances were long, and life was too short to worry. It concerns a rational choice made by a scattered people in a big country. It is about a kind of domestic technology which suggests both the reality and the metaphor of "social mobility."

The automobile makes possible what Theodore White has called the "social politics" of suburbia. It moves people from suburbs to city, from home to employment. Perhaps more important, at least from the viewpoint of women, it makes both domestic and industrial economy possible, often sequentially. It is difficult to get to work or to school or to run a household without the use of the automobile, unless one wishes to give up the options that its use represents. Those options have to do with time, money, and opportunity. Not only does the much-maligned supermarket depend on the automobile but so does the vast system of education now attended by about half the college population. Campuses without dormitories are as dependent on mechanization as, say, most hospitals. Part-time employment often would be impossible without the automobile — and that kind of employment is the last resort of the married woman with children who lives on a split-second schedule. Advertising and technology sell wheels — but they provide access to social life.

The new middle-class population is often described in terms of income, status, or possessions. But it might just as easily be described in terms of time and opportunities. The schedule of the middle-class family now looks like something printed by United Airlines. It is a commutation between social institutions. The old agencies of social life have been replaced by an intricate network of adult classes, recreation centers, community events, sales, and other dispersed forms of consumption. The symbolism of the shopping mall should not be lost: That is now where ballet exhibitions are held, where automobile displays are parked along the mall, where cooking lessons are given, and where general community interests make themselves felt.

In dealing with technology, advertising's function has always been simple, even morally neutral: to sell goods and services. But its affects are never simple. Advertising and the technology it moves have irrevocably changed social life from a steady alternation of work and sleep. The change has been unintended: Henry Ford did not begin to manufacture his cars in order to sell them to his workers — although that is what eventually happened. Advertising did not set out to create a world in which salaries would increase as effort diminished. Yet, that too eventually happened, and the marketing of technology became directly related to some very uncommon historical conditions: the improvement of life for a majority and the appearance of mass leisure.

Advertising is of course responsible for our "culture of consumption," which is every bit as philistine as its critics make out. But that "culture" or framework for human activity does need some historical definition. Slightly over a century ago, the argument for reform in England was based upon the belief that 14 hours of work each day was enough. The opposing argument held that people did not have the moral or imaginative resources to cope with freedom. With the work day now about half that, it can be seen that something else, something once suggested only by mythology of the Golden Age, has intervened. Leisure has become economically significant. More important, it has become a form of freedom.

As the voice of technology, advertising has moved goods which are both labor-saving and labor-intensifying. Heavy domestic goods — furnaces which replace coal, refrigerators which replace ice, washing machines which replace indentured female labor — are examples of the first. The automobile is the best example of the second. Labor-saving devices like the dishwasher create possibilities for labor intensification. They make possible second-job employment by one or both members of a couple.

Second-job employment has had an enormous effect on middle-class American life, and not merely because of what it does for the gross national product. It means, among other things, that housewives enter the economy. It also means that *leisure* ceases to be a synonym for *amusement*. A few years ago, social scientists admitted their astonishment at finding out just how much part-time employment there is in the United States — their working hypothesis had been that an age of leisure implies the *absence* of work. On the contrary, leisure confirms freedom of opportunity. One of the best examples of its use is the most obvious, women freed from the (literally) killing work of farm or household in order to qualify for the marketplace. Domestic and economic life have until very recent times been almost impossible for women to reconcile. Here is a description of a young woman in a 19th-century factory in England from the notes of Friedrich Engels:

> M. H. twenty years old, has two children, the youngest a baby, that is tended by the other, a little older. The mother goes to the mill shortly after five o'clock in the morning, and comes home at eight at night; all day the milk pours from her breasts, so that her clothing drips with it [quoted in Hyman, 1962: 165].

Engels was said to be able to stutter in a dozen languages, but he could think in at least one of them. We have added two variables to history. They are labor-saving and labor-intensifying technology *and the belief that it should be universally available*. Without them, life might well continue on the level suggested by 19th-century experience. The realms of economic and domestic life would be brutally opposed.

As important as technology is the conception that it should be devoted to individual advancement. The economics of everyday life are based upon ideas. When ancient Sparta wished to discourage trade because it was unwarlike, its government supposedly converted all money into lead. The point was simply made: Spartans could neither sit down nor stand up without divesting themselves of their assets. (That is not the story of social mobility, although it has charming possibilities.) Our own economics are based upon productivity, individual aspiration for change, and social utility. These are the things emphasized by advertising. That emphasis is expressed in a number of ways, some morally admirable and others morally indifferent. Advertising has sometimes suggested that production and consumption are ultimate human ends. This not only fails to be moral but also is not even sensible. But advertising also suggests that production and consumption are means, which is a different argument. Our experience forces the conclusion that they raise the standard of living and allow for the discretionary use of time and labor. Productivity creates resources while advertising directs them to consumers in a way that maximizes leisure or the freedom from necessity.

When we talk about users of resources we are necessarily talking about social inclusiveness. The marketplace wants to sell as much as possible to as many as possible. In order to accomplish that it must aim at the kind of individual who represents the group, not at the one who stands apart from it. Both democracy and the marketplace depend on the average man. A famous advertisement once praised "the man of distinction," but that idea is something of an illusion: Advertising in general is far more concerned with his opposite, who is just about completely without distinctions. The matter has been nicely put by Daniel Boorstin, who said in *The Americans* that after the Civil War, advertising "showed an aggressive, sometimes belligerent democracy. . . . For it ruthlessly and relentlessly sought to widen the audience and to broaden its appeal" (1973: 137). In that sense, advertising has done far more than persuade, state, or convey information. It is a kind of declaration of equality. It assumes a mass market. It thrives on tastes which are completely average. It serves the desires of the largest possible number. It certainly attempts to reflect the hopes and fears of the majority and cannot escape identifying itself with them.

NOTES

1. A classic of interdisciplinary study of economics and literature is L. C. Knight's (1937) *Drama & Society in the Age of Jonson*. This book makes the point that Jacobean literature is a mirror of economic events, for example, the tremendous inflation of the early 17th century. Among other things, *Volpone* is a study of the affects of New World gold bullion on traditional European life.

2. This is taken from the Boston *Gazette* of January 26, 1741, and quoted by Mott (1962: 58). The medicine was also said to be good for "the Cholick, Dry Belly-Ach, Loss of Limbs, Fevers and Agues, Asthmas, Coughs, and all sorts of Obstructions, Rheumatism, Sickness at the Stomach."

3. This passage, which needs no further citation, is from the end of the Seven Ages of Man speech in *As You Like It*.

4. See, for example, Mitchell and Deak (1974), Power (1963), and Evans (1969). Evans quotes from a sermon which suggests the impotence of guild regulations:

> The innkeepers and wine merchants secretly mix water with their wine, or bad wine with good. . . . Butchers blow out their meat. Before delivering a pig they drain away its blood and use it to redden the gills of stale and discoloured fish. The drapers. . . . only display their goods in dark streets, so as to deceive the buyers as to its quality. . . . The preacher tells the story of the old customer who asked to have his sausages cheaper as he had dealt only with the one butcher for seven years. "Seven years!" cried the pork-butcher, "and you're still alive!" [1969: 49].

5. See, for example, the recent review of James David Barber's *The Pulse of Politics* by Walter Dean Burnham (1980: 30).

6. For an account at (literary) first-hand, see Twain's (1962: 98-99) *Adventures of Huckleberry Finn*. The King and the Duke are discussing their quack-doctoring past, with the former stooping to admit that he has made a pretty decent trade of it:

> Well, I'd been selling an article to take the tartar off the teeth — and it does take it off, too, and generally the enamel along with it — but I staid about one night longer than I ought to. . . . I've done considerable in the doctoring way in my time. Layin' on o' hands is my best holt — for

cancer, and paralysis, and sich things; and I k'n tell a fortune pretty good, when I've got somebody along to find out the facts for me.

7. Here is Bounderby on labor: "There's not a Hand in this town, Sir, man, woman, or child, but has one ultimate object in life. That object is, to be fed on turtle soup and venison with a gold spoon. Now, they're not a-going — none of 'em — ever to be fed on turtle soup and venison with a gold spoon." His interlocutor "professed himself in the highest degree instructed and refreshed" (Oxford University, 1970: 126).

8. Here is Toynbee's view of educational progress and cultural regression:

> The possibility of turning education to account as a means of amuse-ment for the masses — and of profit for the enterprising persons by whom the amusement is purveyed — has only arisen since the intro-duction of universal elementary education; and this new possibility has conjured up a third stumbling block which is the greatest of all. The bread of universal education is no sooner cast upon the waters than a shoal of sharks arises from the depths and devours the children's bread under the educator's very eyes. In the educational history of England the dates speak for themselves. The edifice of universal elementary education was, roughly speaking, completed by Forster's Act in 1870; and the Yellow Press was invented some twenty years later — as soon, that is, as the first generation of children from the national schools had acquired sufficient purchasing-power [cited in Somervell, 1971: 339].

4

ADVERTISING AND MASS SOCIETY

How are ideas about social life and social change transmitted? So far as advertising is concerned, in certain predictable ways. For example, televised advertisements are idealized reflections of American family and community life. Everyone pictured in advertisements has some kind of happy and productive connection with other people, with jobs, and with social institutions. In order to present that kind of picture, advertisements are often out of date: They show us the kind of social arrangements that were characteristic when we were growing up — or even when our parents were growing up. Advertising is a kind of maneuver between two ideas: the stability and comfort of traditional life and the change and excitement of life in the future. It combines the idea of individual freedom with nostalgia. It not only tells us that consumption will change and improve us but also promises that we will, magically, always stay the same.

THE PROBLEM OF EQUALITY

Since the publication of de Tocqueville's *Democracy in America* we have reflected, often uneasily, on the power and growth of equality. When de Tocqueville stated that America would become ever more equal he was not referring entirely to politics. Ideas would be equally true or at least equally compelling. He early discerned one of the mysteries of American life: the reason why a moralist like Elbert Hubbard could be taken for an equivalent to Emer-

son and why a painter like Norman Rockwell could be
taken for a major artist. If there was not to be a hierarchy of
class there could not be one of style. Under the new
conditions of American democracy the average would become the ideal.

Within the marketplace a new diffusion of wealth
would determine that ideal. Under the old regimes of
Europe the craftsman had had very few options. He was
bound, de Tocqueville (1956: 170) says, to "sell his work-
manship at a high price to the few" because there was no
one else to sell it to. He depended on patrons rather than
on customers. These patrons displayed relatively constant
tastes for the style, durability, and quality of commodities.
They were able to enforce their cultural values upon an
economy.

Under the new conditions of American equality
craftsmen altered their mode of production. They did this
because the marketplace expanded to include great numbers of men with new sources of income. The customers
that de Tocqueville observed in the age of Jackson had a
good deal of money, but not much conception of how to
spend it. They were unsure of themselves even while
anxious to assert their new social power through
consumption.

The phrase that de Tocqueville uses to describe their
social anxieties is revealing: the new market for commodities includes a multitude of men with "passions" for
consumption. In dealing with them — in dealing with what
was essentially a new form of mass psychology — the
craftsman was forced to change his traditional ideas. First
of all, he had to recognize that excellence and durability
were no longer important. In a democracy, what matters
most is that the use of commodities should reflect equal-

ity. The following is a very useful metaphor about democratic culture:

> When none but the wealthy had watches, they were almost all very good ones: few are now made which are worth much, but everybody has one in his pocket [1956: 171].

de Tocqueville did not pursue one implication: that the craftsman might eventually depend on a middleman to articulate social taste. Stating the ideal of the average would itself become an industry.

In a democracy like America the object of production would necessarily come to be selling commodities "at a low price to all." de Tocqueville, in a sense, predicted the advent of Henry Ford. And he predicted something larger, the advent of a new set of cultural ideas and mechanisms. They were to determine the growth of mass society, with every man a potential customer, and the growth of mass culture, with every man a potential audience.

The good news is that mass society includes a great many people who would never before have been thought of as being essential to the *civitas*. The great flaw of 19th-century industrialism had been that the uneducated, the unemployed, and the unproductive were outside most social institutions. Dickens's *Hard Times* shows us that the factory was the only connection that workers had to civic life, because chapels did not foster religion, unions did not work, and schools did not educate. *Bleak House* shows us poverty without remedy and *Oliver Twist* shows us workhouses which were worse than the conditions they were trying to cure.

The masses were unable to participate in society and formed what Marx called a "proletariat" or group with no real function in national life. But the "masses," a term common both to Marx and to the lines inscribed on the base of the statue of Liberty, have now become the middle class. The "masses" now hold most of the jobs in America, consume the most goods, and provide government with most of its revenue.

The remarkable thing about the American middle class is not its standard of living but its extent. It is the majority. History has sometimes extended the benefits of prosperity, but almost never to a majority. That is all good news. The bad news is that mass society expresses itself through mass culture: the majority's ideas, dreams, values, beliefs, and aesthetics. The forms of high culture are books, symphonies, and paintings; those of mass culture are comic strips, movies, and television. Dominating all of mass culture is a social institution that provides the objects of its imagination: advertising.

Mass culture was already an issue when Matthew Arnold remarked in his essay on "Democracy" that an uneducated and unreflective middle class might soon dominate England's national life. Newly enriched by trade, they would be in the position to replace older elites. Like the new men descried by de Tocqueville, they would have a good deal more money than taste. And they could be expected to use that money in order to define their social lives. What would be the likely effect of replacing tradition by money? The new class would transform and lower social life: "They will certainly *Americanise* it. They will rule it by their energy, but they will deteriorate it by their low ideals and want of culture" (Arnold, 1962: 464). Arnold's essay on "Democracy" was published in 1861; since then the debate over mass culture has been one of the great issues of intellectual life. It influenced the writings and affected the lives of Henry James, T.S. Eliot, and Ezra Pound. It animated the criticism of H.L. Mencken and Van Wyck Brooks. It absorbed the work of the early Marx on alienation and provided a thesis, in the work of Hannah Arendt, for the role of the masses under fascism. Needless to say, high culture has been hostile to its counterpart. I think that Randolph Bourne's summary holds good even today for making that point:

> the flotsam and jetsam of American life, the downward undertow of our civilization with its leering cheapness and falseness of taste, and spiritual outlook, the absence of mind and sincere feeling which we see in our slovenly towns, our vapid moving pictures, our popular novels, and in the vacuous faces of the crowds on the city streets. . . . This is the cultural wreckage of our time [1920: 281].

The critique of mass culture became a subgenre of American literature; from Nathanael West to Tom Wolfe our men of letters have tried to plumb the shallows of majority taste.

UNDERSTANDING MASS CULTURE

There are of course many "cultures" within the United States. There is the entirely separate culture of Amish enclaves, the famously separated two cultures of science and of humanities noted by C. P. Snow, and the self-consciously new "youth culture," "drug culture," and "rock culture." There seems to be an irresistible urge in American criticism to dignify, ennoble, and enlarge whatever it deals with. Mass culture probably contains a little of every other kind of "culture" that comes to mind. Those who have analyzed, criticized, praised, or blamed it have used four general categories: they have argued about style, standards, human nature, and democratic values. It is not likely that we will understand the critique of advertising, or advertising itself, without understanding their debate. Advertising is the largest object descried within the world of mass culture.

Those who assert the values of style understand mass culture to be the expression of the majority in subintellectual and sub-artistic form. It is the sum total of rock music and *True Confessions,* of *The Gong Show* and Citizen's Band, of beach buggies and bumper stickers. Its attitudes are bad enough — but its commodities are worse. It is all commercialized: fast food, drive-ins, the constant jingle of advertisements. Sometimes the critic will briefly consecrate soul food or country music or the Roller Derby as signs of the times. But from the viewpoint of style, mass culture is defined by its vulgarity, hedonism, and above all its materialism.

The connection with advertising already becomes apparent. So far as the critic is concerned, which is to say so far as the educated and critical sensibility discerns, advertising makes mass culture possible. It is associated with the *commodities* of mass culture like automobiles and all-too-portable stereos; with the *agencies* of mass culture like television; and with the underlying *mode* of mass culture, consumption.

There is one other important aspect to the argument of style. One of the great themes of modern life is disenchantment with others in society. It is a theme of alienated art, literature, and politics. The moral of Ibsen's *An Enemy of the People* has become that of our century: "The majority *never* has right on its side. Never, I say! That is one of those social lies against which an independent, intelligent man must wage war." The paradox of democracy is that it provides equality but makes no provision for difference. To *become* middle class, like Fitzgerald's Myrtle Wilson, is a dream of change through consumption. To *remain* middle class, however, is a nightmare. An industry that never stops trying to find common ground in all motives, whose images and copy immortalize the average, will necessarily be perceived as Ibsen perceived the majority.[1]

Standards or their absence constitute a second theme in the critique of mass culture. Dwight Macdonald (1961: 78) summed up his study of *Masscult & Midcult* with a remark from Kierkegaard: "Even a drunken sailor exhibiting a peep-show has dialectically the same right to a public as the greatest man."[2] *Masscult & Midcult* finds the worst characteristic of mass culture to be equality: *I Love You Truly* is as good as Shubert, Liberace is as good as Serkin, and Norman Rockwell is as good as Picasso. We are reminded of de Tocqueville, who foresaw that society without differences of class would promote arts without differences of style — and of Ibsen, who hated the whole idea.

There is a good deal to Macdonald's argument — the Bureau of the Census has published statistics indicating that by 1976 about a million people described themselves as artists by occupation (see Berman, 1979: 48). The self-ascription does not mean that anything was created or sold. It only means that their hopes were artistic. Hobbies, crafts, and the amusements of the retired become equal to traditional forms of art because it is easier to redefine terms, standards, and ideas than it is to disappoint cultural expectations. Government becomes involved in this process as these enormous numbers of self-defined artists become an important political constituency: The National Endowment for the Arts makes their definition of work its own.

I would judge that the greatest animus of *Masscult & Midcult* is against media. Hollywood, magazines, book publishers, and Madison Avenue are all implicated for their debasement of ideas and feelings. They are all in the business of promoting the false values and standards of mass society. Macdonald is particularly concerned by the shift from the criterion of objective judgment to that of simple popularity. Because advertising dreads the first and exemplifies the second, it is centrally involved in the guilt of mass culture. And, of course, it sustains the media, which are more interested in roller-skating horses than in Renoir.

In ascending order of moral seriousness we come to the third critique of mass culture, its revelation of human motives. Ernest Van den Haag has been one of the most influential writers on this theme, and here is what he has to say about the relationship of mass culture to mass nature:

> The mass of men dislikes and always has disliked learning and art. It wishes to be distracted from life rather than to have it revealed; to be comforted by traditional (possibly happy and sentimental) tropes, rather than to be upset by new ones. It is true that it wishes to be thrilled, too. But irrational violence or vulgarity provides thrills, as well as release, just as sentimentality provides escape. [1961: 59].

Van den Haag's often-cited essay appeared over 20 years ago. Since then there has been every conceivable form of consciously planned, institutionally financed, publicly distributed amusement of violence and disgust. It is almost as if mass culture had conspired to prove his point.

Within 10 years of Van den Haag's essay, magazines were printing advertisements for whips and chains; and newspapers were running illustrations of movies that used them. Within 15 years horror movies had become a new phenomenon, developing from an early history of challenging the imagination to their current practice of extending the limits of disgust. Within 20 years "festivals" or "concerts" had appeared which were based upon the pleasures of deviance. Slam dancing, or gangs charging each other on the dance floor, leaving mounting piles of the wounded, bleeding, and unconscious, are now social events. The account of a witness is useful, if unconsciously ironic:

> "Sure, there was violence before," said one longtime punk scene-maker who preferred not to be identified, "but it was more like play-acting violence, like guerilla theater. Now we get these crazy, pathetic jerks who just want to get some cheap thrill" ["The 'punk rock' scene turns to bloody violence," 1980: A-18].

The passage suggests a number of things: the translation of respectability from the 1960s which had endowed art with violence; the credentials of connoisseurs of punk; the conception that disgust is a form of "art" or "theater" when rightly represented; the recognition, inter alia, that there are subtleties and styles even in sadism.

Mass culture has, in some of its forms, proceeded through induced toleration. Woodstock was made possible by the symbolic relationship of drugs, music, and pacifism; but successive events, each more violent than the last, have had other ends in view.

The three critiques that I have summarized share certain beliefs. One is that the majority wants what it gets and gets what it wants. To that extent, the critics take the same position as that famously taken by General Motors about consumers. Another belief is that media are centrally responsible for the worst effects of mass culture. In part, that is self-evident: "Concerts," "festivals," and other public events are advertised, communicated and reviewed. After they are over they become news. Yet a third belief is that media have themselves become socially regressive or disruptive — as Morris Janowitz points out in The Last Half-Century, "the popular culture content of the mass media, particularly the emphasis on violence, has a long-term effect" on both "social personality" and "personal controls" (1978: 329).

The fourth view of mass culture is something of a corrective. Herbert J. Gans has given up on distinctions in his book *Popular Culture and High Culture*. He believes that in a society as large and various as our own, we will simply have to accommodate "cultural pluralism." The uneducated have their culture and critics have another; everyone else finds a level in between. Compromises are for the most part unsatisfying, but this one seems to have the virtue of realism: There is not much one can do about the *de facto* distribution of styles, tastes, and tolerances in the United States. There is another point, made by Edward Shils, about the actual nature of mass society. It is completely unlike this view held of it by intellectuals:

> A territorially extensive society, with a large population, highly urbanized and industrialized. Power is concentrated in this society, and much of the power takes the form of manipulation of the mass through the media of mass communication. Civic spirit is low, local loyalties are few, primordial solidarity is virtually nonexistent. There is no individuality, only a restless and frustrated egoism. It is like the state of nature described by Thomas Hobbes, except that public disorder is restrained through the manipulation of the elite and the apathetic idiocy of the mass [1975: 92].

The realities are for Shils somewhat different. Intellectuals may be alienated, but the mass cannot be described in terms quite so perfectly theoretical. What strikes him is the consensuality of mass culture. Our large, complex, and mass society works — and works rather well at that. It has held together, even in difficult times, in families and communities. It has managed the contradictory task of providing individual choice while maintaining common institutions.

In his conception, the most notable characteristic of our mass society is its peacefulness. It recognizes human rights and may be said even to further their development. Mass culture may be vulgar, but mass society has not become authoritarian.

Our own experience suggests that Shils is largely correct. I take the word *experience* literally: Those whom we meet daily who drive buses or taxis, who repair faucets or broken bones are not only more complex but also a good deal more impressive than the term *mass* implies. It may be that Will Rogers was making more than one kind of joke when he said that he never met a man he did not like. Perhaps he was thinking not of the pieties of smalltown life but of the pieties of intellectual discourse.

WHAT COMMERCIALS DO

The following outlines the relationship of advertising to mass democratic society. It covers the process of consumption; advertising as a socializing institution; the idea of change in an industrial culture; and the language of social change. I have begun with consumption because nothing has more engaged the critics of advertising and of mass culture.

Advertisements are often materialistic and sensate; and they debase those values which are associated with commodities. Love, friendship, and family life become trivialized, the objects of false emotions. But consumption involves more than the display of vulgarity over acquisitions. It is part of a process beginning with the discovery of resources and ending with the utilization of goods or services. One of the objects of that process certainly is profit. Another is the reinforcement of the social system through which the economy works. There are some general themes to modern advertising; and they are probably

more visible and more important than the praise of goods
or services. One of these states that technology works for
the largest possible number of people: It is a mode of
mass society. The second states that consumption expresses legitimate human desires: It is a mode of mass
culture. The third states that innovation is a natural consequence of modern life. If other institutions sufficiently
strong had remained to us they would be stating these
themes or commenting on them. But institutions decline
and are replaced: We have, for example, gone from
church to school to television in the last half-century in the
search for authoritative guidance in the "small morals" or
habits of everyday life.

Commercials and other forms of product advertising
are not so much inducements to buy goods as they are
statements about why goods are produced, whom they
benefit, and how they fit into our lives. Advertising reas-
sures consumers that they are the reason for consumption. For example, General Motors, once notorious for
believing that what was good for itself was good for the
United States, now advertises a different kind of ideology.
Its commercials depict "people building transportation
for people." There is no salestalk for automobiles. Instead,
we see a vision of social integration. The camera is on the
workers, who are its real subject: forming a spectrum of
male and female, black and white, old and young. They
represent the productive middle class, and their enterprise is the common good.

We all recognize the public tone of commercials and
other forms of advertisement, a tone indistinguishable
from that of political oration. The term *people* now so
much in use by General Motors appears interminably in
the speeches of former President Carter. Its use legiti-
mates political or entrepreneurial intentions, suggesting a
public good for every private end. And indeed, American
institutions are devoted to that kind of language. Banks

advertise the public benefit of savings rather than the private necessity of loans. Insurance companies flood the mails with sensible diets and habits designed to lengthen life: These advertisements are designed not to attract customers but to speak *pro bono publico*. Even oil companies advertise restraint, and a "self-sufficiency" that suggests far more than the end of reliance on OPEC. The world depicted by advertising, and through its efforts, relies on superego institutions.

The context of commercials, especially for mass society, is at least as important as their primary message. Commercials delineate a social world. Within that world, social values are upheld more firmly than in our own world. The social unit is the household. Although the national divorce rate now approaches that of marriage, this household is threatened only by acts of nature. It is surrounded, in this Malthusian age, by children and grandparents. The young are not insubordinate. Settings are often rural or suburban — although we live for the most part in cities. Characters seem to have a wide circle of acquaintance — although the great theme of high culture fiction, criticism, and even movies is alienation. Families are absorbed by social tasks. People get advice from each other, not from psychiatrists. Society is cohesive and needs no rule of law or lawyers.

In short, mass society is orderly and self-sustaining. It is reminded of this through the advertisement of consumption of idealized rather than actual historical circumstances. It is no wonder that Varda Leymore has written of advertising's ability to create a mythology. She was, of course, speaking in nonmetaphorical terms: emphasizing the relationship of advertisements to the eternal facts of sustaining life by eating, drinking, and membership in a tribe. To use the term *mythological* in a slightly more metaphorical way, I would judge that it has a social rather than an existential form. Advertisements are related to imagination in the way that utopias relate to literature.

Happy families are all alike. At the time when de Tocqueville was writing about our social mores, *The Ladies Book* (1830) knew the reason why:

> See, she sits, she walks, she speaks, she looks — unutterable things! Inspiration springs up in her very paths — it follows her footsteps. A halo of glory encircles her, and illuminates her whole orbit. With her, man not only feels safe, but actually renovated [quoted in Skolnick, 1980: 119].

The combination of femininity and perfection, long to haunt the American imagination, became a stock part of 19th-century social theory. It was finally the novelists from Mark Twain to Ernest Hemingway who polished off this culture figure by creating women in a new incarnation: man-eaters, every one of them. When Brett Ashley, Daisy Buchanan, and Eula Varner appeared on the literary scene, perfection had pretty much run its course — except, one notes, for advertising. High culture looks ahead, hence the *avant garde*. Mass culture, to coin a utopian phrase, is always looking backward.

The world of television commercials is just about 20 years out of date in its social arrangements. It hearkens back not only to earlier times but to different circumstances. It persists in showing households with cleaning women and little general stores staffed by eccentric experts. It shows the American family (at a time when all three candidates for the Presidency are actively deploring its decadence) as it has traditionally been viewed, from Victorian to early modern times. What is missing from the advertised view of family experience are all those statistical evils that social science has so carefully enumerated: rising promiscuity, divorce, adolescent sexuality, the prevalence of drugs among both adolescents and adults, the universal experience of crime, and the new mass occurrence of venereal disease and bastardy. Add to this, hunger, want, and unemployment. What has replaced experience as we know it — or rather as we apprehend it through the *other* agencies of media — is a construct of mass society flourishing despite necessary evils. In the world of commercials, men are employed and women are coping with the demands of both tradition and liberation. Life is organized and purposeful. Relatives are provided for; and family, community, and nation exist within meaningful relationships. A society is depicted that conforms to the ideals of mass culture. It does so even at the cost of ignoring reality. On the other hand, perhaps reality is viewed that way by those who experience it.

Mass society as depicted by advertising has the capacity to adjust to social change. Daniel Bell has written that "mass consumption meant the acceptance, in the crucial area of life-style, of the idea of social change and personal transformation" (1976: 66). Sometimes change works through vast ideas or great historical events; more often it accumulates through daily experience. And our own daily experience has been that of a marketplace in which changes of status and even of self are readily available. In that sense, consumption literally *is* change.

In that respect, advertising may be quite right about its view of reality. I have mentioned the work of Lipset and Bendix, which concludes that the possession of goods elevates us socially. It makes us indistinguishable from others who own them, no matter what their education or genealogy may be. The argument may be said to apply, within limits, to personal consumption. Cosmetics, dress, and other forms of acquired style change people and society. The effect varies: When I asked the president of one of our most influential agencies for an example of advertising's affect on society he remarked, with no irony, that deodorants had made travel by subway possible. True enough. There is nothing so illustrative of inchoate mass society as a crowded subway — but the notion of each

individual superego conforming to the idea of inoffen-
siveness does give one critical pause. Even a mob has
preconceptions about style.

The Great Gatsby — the great American novel for this
century — is fascinated by this idea of style. Myrtle Wilson
is more or less the spirit of mass consumption:

> "My dear," she cried, "I'm going to give you this dress as
> soon as I'm through with it. I've got to get another one
> tomorrow. I'm going to make a list of all the things I've
> got to get. A massage and a wave, and a collar for the
> dog, and one of those cute little ashtrays where you
> touch a spring, and a wreath with a black silk bow for
> mother's grave that'll last all summer. I got to write down
> a list so I won't forget all the things I got to do."

Her desires (perhaps de Tocqueville's phrase "passions"
ought to be recalled) are devoted to change, to becoming
middle-class. She has read every magazine and advertisement in New York and knows how one becomes a lady.
Gatsby's social imagination, like Myrtle's comes from the
media of mass culture. Both have read the literature of
success, from Horatio Alger to *Town Tattle*. Both actually
believe that new shirts or pink suits or an automobile that
looks like a band box — or a new apartment, new friends,
new dog, and new lover — constitutes the American
Dream. Consumption, at least, is commensurate to their
capacity to wonder.

Advertising, then, creates a social world in many respects superior to our own. Consumption elevates one
into it. When we speak of social change we are thinking
really of the infinite number of changes that occur for
individuals. In the aggregate, social change consists of the
new conceptions of self that are fed by advertising and
consumption. For Myrtle Wilson, a massage and a wave
and a collar for the dog represent social mobility. They are

services and acquisitions of the middle class. But, once in the middle class many of us can hardly wait to get out. High style is a continuous attack on middle-class complacency. Advertising has the difficult task of portraying a nirvana of consumption while suggesting its transcendence. Half a century after Myrtle Wilson comes the Jordache look: "Hot. Sexy. Irresistible. If you've got it, show us." Every phrase is of course ambiguous. The illustration, between *avant garde* and pornography, shows a half-naked woman mounted on the back of a half-naked man. Both face away from the camera. Both are masked; the man is epicene and the woman sadistically in control; incredibly tight jeans, the object of it all, show brilliantly to advantage. There is more than one social theme. Consumption not only liberates us from our tiresome middle-class selves but also is capable of operating in a realm of absolute freedoms. Aldous Huxley did a definitive job on this theme in *Brave New World*.

Christopher Lasch's *The Culture of Narcissism* is about the breakdown of social stability caused by advertising's slavery to change. Marcuse's *One-Dimensional Man* is about the role advertising plays in protecting the capitalist sensibility. It may be that both are quite right.

Consumption — better put, the delineation of a self by acquisition — is guided both by stasis and by change. Broadly speaking, televised advertising represents stasis, even if it exists in an adversary relationship with the programming that it supports. Magazine and newspaper advertising, aimed at rather more select constituencies of mass society, speak more to change. In part this has to do with the nature of commodities, in part with that of constituencies. Television sells bread, frozen dinners, washing machines, and soap. Its commodities are extremely basic. They are pumped up desperately full of virtues, but soap is soap. All it can do is clean; it cannot move one into the upper class. But high style will do that — those Jordache jeans suggest the abandonment of bourgeois self and attachment to a class apart. Advertising provides both the guidelines to bourgeois life and to a life beyond it. The genres are sometimes confused — one finds change momentarily exalted by Hamburger Helper and nostalgia temporarily enshrined at Bloomingdale's — but the two kinds of message are in general reinforced by the appropriate media. We learn from consumption how to be ideal citizens and how to transcend our origins through our desires.

WHERE COMMERCIALS TAKE PLACE

The histories of advertising often point out that salesmanship as an art and vocation ended with the growth of media. Among the first of the new modes of advertising were Sears, Roebuck catalogs which replaced not only salesmen but also their stores. Later and ever-newer modes of advertising like television have replaced things we have long thought to be even more fundamental. Our social history has been marked by the emergence and disappearance of institutions, which is one of the reasons for our cultural anxiety. The source of civic authority was once the community, which, like Mark Twain's Hannibal or Sinclar Lewis' Zenith or Sherwood Anderson's Winesburg, Ohio, formed a complete (and sometimes oppressive) social system. But the community is now a suburb or extension of a larger organism. It has very little authority over private life. Authority over social values, once possessed by communal associations, has been absorbed by other sources. One is the federal government; another the agencies of literacy. Advertising in particular has taken on advisory functions once held by the little platoons of everyday life.

The interesting thing about this is what might be called the piety of social form. The advice that television bestows comes from a cast of communal characters. Commercials are in effect cultural psychodramas, with enormous amounts of advice given by cleaning women, plumbers, friends, acquaintances, relatives, doctors, clerks, and other fictionalized members of a traditional American community. That community passed away over a generation ago, but the confusion over history is intentional. Since the community no longer exists, it must be invented — or restored. It is in the name of older communal values like thrift that we are advised to make certain purchases. There is a powerful suggestion that the old American community does exist, somewhere out there, and that its members are actively judging the consumer by what she does for herself and for her family.

The fictitious community of televised advertising has many more human relationships than those ordinarily experienced in urban life. The advice we get is of two orders: one half is voiced on behalf of kitchen cleansers, washing machines, and deodorants; the other half has to do with habits, values, and anxieties. The audience learns, for example, that a daughter who knows more about improved Whisk than her mother may well be more knowledgeable about other things. And indeed, one great theme of commercials is the superior social knowledge of the younger generation. Since they have discretionary income that is to be expected. It is also to be expected that advertising will emphasize a major theme for them, the direct experience of social change through consumption. Commercials tell us a good deal about acquired style.

There is a wonderful example of this socializing role in the ad *Esquire* recently ran in *The New York Times:*

> Society is changing its definitions of manhood at too rapid a rate, leaving the man in the middle.
>
> Esquire understands this.
>
> And it intends to help with the problem, in an important, meaningful way.
>
> But it will do even more.
>
> Because in the midst of all this unsettling change, a man is still expected to know what wrench to use, what to wear for each occasion, what wine to order, how to make important decisions about his life, how to entertain a woman, where to vacation, and how to buy a stereo system that sounds like a concert hall.
>
> He's supposed to learn all of this automatically, by osmosis.
>
> Esquire knows better.[3]

There are several functions that this fulfills, the simplest being to give those who have joined the middle class some idea of how to think, behave, and consume. It acknowledges that we no longer pick up values "automatically." It acknowledges, that is to say, that certain social institutions are dead. The tactics call for this sort of recognition, for a mass culture version of a great social problem over which we may agonize. Mass culture is mimetic, and this, like the *Merv Griffin Show*, treats issues of stupendous importance with the same attentiveness given by a monkey to a banana. *Esquire* also understands the attractions of anxiety as a social commodity. If you can afford to subscribe and to buy that stereo, you deserve prosperity with the curse taken off it — purchasing power refined by insecurity. The language suggests Arnold's new middle class, poised between economic power and cultural ignorance. And, although the ad is about wine, women, and song, it treats them as if they were commodities available only through consumption. In a sense, opinion about them is also a commodity.

Media sustained by advertising define activities and legitimize interests for their readers: In that respect *Esquire* acts for one branch of the middle class in the same way that the *New Yorker* does for another. Through advertisements in both we receive an enormous amount of *silent* information: how to act in relation to people, possessions, and ourselves.

Advertisement — especially in the form of televised commercials — has by now taken on moral authority as well as authority over style. A very interesting chapter in Jonathan Price's book about commercials, *The Best Thing on TV*, charts the extent of social feelings they display. His thesis is that commercials "simply underline our society's unconscious mental life" (1978: 45). That mental life is not centered on sexuality, but rather on recollections of the past. A more authentic world lies behind the nostalgia of commercials, a world of psychological and of cultural childhood. As Price puts it, Mom sells: "Nostalgia for home, memories of childhood, a kid's longing for love from Mom and Grandma, these outsell the urge for sex and the itch for violence. . . . To judge from commercials, it is Mom who best cajoles, argues, charms, and scares us into buying" (1978: 44). Mythology, as always, is based upon reality.

Silent information accompanies every sale. Campbell's soup ads tell us that motherhood is eternally protective. Pan Am brings to mind the relatives we have left behind in the old country. Bell Telephone connects us with the aged. The theme that connects all of these is the separation that life has imposed. To joke about the American way of death is to forget that commercials take it rather seriously. Change of course must culminate in death. One much-awarded commercial from Hallmark is literally about this transition: It shows the eviction of Grandma as the moment arrives for her to leave the family home for a solitary apartment. She is seen surrounded by the memories and debris of years past, telling her grandson what they mean. Price remarks that he has seen this commercial three times and cried over it each time. Ron Hoff, one of the writers responsible for it, explains the effect: "All middle-aged people feel guilty about their parents. . . . The family is changing. . . . It's the end of childhood" (Price, 1978: 46). And in fact the commercial is about social necessity that becomes a trauma in all our lives, as the extended family is replaced by the nuclear family.

This commercial is perhaps more moving as a historical metaphor than as a vignette. The old house — it may be America itself — is full of the good things of the past, which take the shape of unusable memories. There are three generations: the grandmother who is leaving and will die; the mother who pretends that everything is fine; and the grandson who is the consciousness of the piece, the mystified witness to social change. But Hallmark can make it no more endurable than Boethius.

Other commercials do try to make social change palatable. As I have noted, they portray a world at least one generation out of date; in which there is an extended family; in which cleaning women give good work and good advice; and in which plumbers and physicians willingly make house calls. There is an alternative strategy, to acknowledge the end of the old unities and suggest replacements for them. One replacement is the family of man. A commercial for *ABC Eyewitness News* shows the crew going to a Puerto Rican social club in the quest for social truth. The crew is hesitant about entering a strange and frankly dangerous place. Suddenly,

> A fat Latin woman waves, "Hello, Roger Grimsby." She crosses to him and sweeps him up to dance. Soon they are all dancing together. Ah, humanity [Price, 1978: 54].

The theme of universal brotherhood is addressed by many other commercials. Fuji Film shows a Japanese family at a Little League game and reminds the audience that "People are pretty much the same all over when it comes to taking pictures." Georgia-Pacific specializes in barn-raisings for which "Friends come from miles around to help." McDonald's and Coca-Cola have, in their missionary way, larger ends in view: "to teach the world to sing in perfect harmony." Universalism is a 20th-century creed, allowing us some relief from the guilt we feel at having lost the ties of family and community, freeing us from the necessity of actually having to involve ourselves in human relationships.

I think it can be said that advertising suggests new social relationships to accommodate new realities. It is not only about cleanliness but about ethnic equality, reverence for the past, and the values of our civil religion. And it is about new and ultimate stages or rites of transition. That Hallmark ad ends with the grandmother leading the boy downstairs. The message of this particular medium is that change comes as inexorably as death.

WHAT COMMERCIALS SAY

The failure of the hairpin industry after Irene Castle bobbed her hair was a story often told in the lore of advertising. Manufacturers had expected women to remain forever long-haired and sentimental, as they had been described by O. Henry in "The Gift of the Magi." But, along came the 1920s and the great hairpin depression. Heroines of consumption like Irene Castle replaced heroines of sensibility like Louisa May Alcott. The new role model gave no one locks of her hair. F. Scott Fitzgerald took a subject closely related to O. Henry's, but made something very different out of it. He throws more light on the subject of bobbed hair — and the cultural history that implied — than many years worth of market research. His short story "Bernice Bobs Her Hair" (1920) is about social change through consumption — and incidentally about the advent of modernism in America. The heroine, an innocent from the Midwest, is being initiated into the higher sophistication by her cousin:

> "Oh, please don't quote *Little Women!*" cried Marjorie impatiently. "That's out of style."
> "You think so?"
> "Heavens, yes! What modern girl could live like those inane females?"
> "They were the models for our mothers."
> Marjorie laughed.
> "Yes, they were — not! Besides, our mothers were all very well in their way, but they know very little about their daughters' problems."

After this dialogue, and a good deal of agonizing, Bernice goes to the edge of all her *Little Women* values and takes the fatal step. She cuts her hair short, becoming "modern" with the very act. The hairpin, used in case studies of market research, may be a humble part of our intellectual history. And Fitzgerald's last interchange between the two girls captures one of the earliest advertising themes: the contrast between tradition and change exemplified by that between mother and daughter.

Advertising is concerned with making the "modern" intelligible to a large mass audience. We recall that in his summary of *The Last Half-Century*, Morris Janowitz writes about the first two modern themes of advertising, production and consumption, being joined by a third: "the management of interpersonal relations." Advertising transmits views about the relationship of society and the self. There is a conscious timeliness to commercials which are attuned to conservation or productivity. Weyerhauser and Texaco attempt to take part in a national dialogue on resources; Clairol suggests that older women should return to work; deodorants, on another level of seriousness, strive desperately to find some new significance in parts of the body unloved by art.

Techniques of advertising are limited by its audience. Mass society is semiliterate: Most people do not read a book from one end of the year to the other. Mass culture, which is the culture we have, goes to movies not to libraries. It is more difficult to get into a movie than it is to get into a museum, although the price is higher. Mass culture is satisfied with few ideas. That is one of the reasons why ads in the *New Yorker* seem interesting when compared to commercials about the same products. Mass advertising works within especially narrow limits when it conveys social change.

Commercials depict mass society in two essential ways: organizing itself around industrial life and responding to the pressures of that life. Beer commercials are quintessential, showing these conceptions in repeated detail. They begin routinely by depicting work as it is generally experienced, in the form of manual labor. The man of beer commercials is *homo faber,* engaged in proving his descent. Work is romanticized, just as it is by the tractor realism of the Soviet Union. Hardhats do representative rather than typical work; using giant earthmovers or bringing down sequoias or doing other things which are heroic rather than laborious. They are associated with machines as Marinetti saw them in *The Futurist Manifesto:* immense power in sculptured form. Beer commercials often take place at sunset after the mastery of nature. They end in a tableau of realized social tranquility.

Commercials for women are much less sure of themselves. They draw the irritation of both conservatives and liberals because of ambiguity displayed toward the acceptance of social change or resistance to it. Women in commercials are torn between past and future. They represent both personal liberation and true belief in traditional family arrangements. What little analysis there is of women in commercials is deeply divided: Behavioristic studies conclude that women are sexually exploited while impressionistic ones find that they continue to represent maternal authority. If the latter is true, then nostalgia is not all it is cracked up to be:

> At first people are aware of tender moments — they long to feel love and comfort. They dream of togetherness — in the family, on the block, in the larger political community. But many people remember undercurrents of guilt, fear, rage, and depression running through years of childhood: and evidently one way for these people to go "home" is to reexperience these emotions [Price, 1978: 44].

"Traditional" women in commercials are threatening; like our mothers they enforce household discipline. They are often more homely and vulgar than in our actual experience. Loud, screechy, and nosy, they seem to exaggerate both the behavior and superego of the middle class. But the stridency and vulgarity may be intended to arouse specific feelings. I think that these manifestations of superego behavior are meant to be associated with the magical powers of consumption. One reason why women in commercials are given the powers and appearance of the wicked witch of the west in *The Wizard of Oz* is that they are avatars of maternal authority. They whine a good deal and are subject to nervous collapse. They invoke ideals in intolerable ways. Even when they are black they are all Jewish mothers, at least as imagined by Phillip Roth or Bruce Jay Friedman. The implication of many commercials celebrating family life is that tradition is warfare carried on by other means.

"New" women express social change through sexuality, not unmediated sexuality: The new woman is not the *Cosmopolitan* girl. She may be a stewardess whose attraction is due in part to her role. Or, she may be a lawyer, judge, or doctor. In any case her body is repressed rather than exposed by what she wears. Authority is a tailored suit. One of the oldest devices in movie-making has been adapted for commercials: Heavy-framed eyeglasses everywhere indicate the covering of sexuality by discipline. When they are taken off it reminds us of Michael Caine in *The Ipcress File* who uses them for everything but going to bed. Authority matters as much for the new woman as for the old. In one commercial, the woman who meets an old friend or lover at a bar and treats him to a Michelob is spectacularly beautiful, but a parody of businesslike assertiveness. She manages to become ugly through her raw voice and mannerisms. We are reminded of *Network*, in which Faye Dunnaway, not too symbolically, takes the superior position in sexual intercourse.

Sexual activity is not the subject of commercials, although sexual innuendo is. But it is sexual identity that seems to matter most. The new woman in commercials is Gloria Steinem under control. Even in that most sublimely dopey of all commercials, in which men wear English Leather or nothing at all, the point is social change. The woman who tells us all about men wearing nothing at all is stylish and aggressive, possibly educated. Her body is nothing to sneeze at — but the message is about her social imagination. Sequential sexuality is part of a larger cultural life which runs without the constraints of tradition. She wills her own experience. In other words, the accent is not on "nothing at all" but on "all my men": a cultural possessive.

The role of women, at least at this cultural moment, is unavoidably schizophrenic. The traditional woman is absorbed in small problems which, like getting shirt collars decently clean, symbolize larger social issues. The triumph over disorder is an assertion of the household's existence. The subdued hysteria running through commercials — desperate shrillness, fear of failure, reliance on others — attests to the reality of whatever experience is depicted. It is not that Tide arouses love, but that the silent anxiety of managing a household is articulated.

There are two kinds of drama of social change on television. The minidrama of commercials is exemplary, showing the average man or woman in familiar situations. The man moves from work to family to well-earned idleness. The woman, if she is traditional, copes with the neolithic realities of food, dirt, and children. New women in commercials find themselves in bar-rooms, airplanes, and courtrooms. They combine sexual desirability with a forbidding kind of authority: Perhaps they are motherhood under a slightly different aspect. Neither men nor women refer to books or ideas. They have no politics. Whatever race or religion they have is indifferent. That is to say, nothing constitutes a difference: All mothers, including black mothers, are Jewish mothers. In the low drama of commercials, people work out their lives within relationships that actually obtain for the majority. Whether or not there is magic or fantasy in their web, these relationships dominate the plot: The actors are always brought back to the improvement of their social life. As an art form, commercials are an expensive mixture of tractor realism, Biedermayer, and Kitsch. They take the dominant art form of mass culture, photography, and apply it to a single subject.

Commercials exist in an adversary relationship to the programming they support. Shows do not have to sell anything or confine themselves to a single subject. The genre they spring from is movies, which everyone knows consciously or not, and they are governed by different expectations. Shows are reviewed by critics and have to account for themselves. When they deal in social change, a national dialogue ensues like that I have mentioned about *One Day at a Time*. But criticism tends to be fairly crude because it is conducted by the media themselves. The media notice the reactionary Archie Bunker and the liberated Ann Romano but not much else. It looks for large social issues, issues that are visible to mass society. These issues concern principles, selves, and relationships — but almost never ideas, art, books, or style. That is why even the best criticism of programming is so dull. Of course, it is limited by what it has to work with.

All televised fiction is the same. Police, western or science-fiction shows have the same characters and use the same devices. The suspect on the ranch or in the courthouse or on the spaceship has a psychological problem dating back to a childhood trauma. Even soap opera has become Freudian, and its dozens of characters are forever at war with themselves. The same moral discussions take place on a desert island or on top of a skyscraper. The limits of ideas and relationships in mass society drive writers obsessively to new *forms*. But there is no escape — no matter how complicated or sensational the plot turns out to be, no matter how many barriers there are between cathexis and satisfaction, the same realm of experience endures. Televised complexity is like reading a comic-book underwater.

The perpetually new forms of programming do try very hard to deal with social change. In part that is because sex and violence have lost some of their utility. Government and critics have placed limits on sex and violence, limits which have been adopted by self-censorship. Social change fascinates television for other reasons, however. Media in America can perceive only change. The definition of "policy" is a necessary political idea that will solve an urgent social problem. As far as the media are concerned, nothing that simply *is* is self-justifying. Aside from constituting news, social change embodies the often-illusory idea of progress.

Daytime television is tied to statistical change. Almost no one on quiz shows is over 35. Such shows are an affirmation of demography. They recognize that the population of this country now has a low median age and they play to the expectations of the statistical majority. By the end of the century they will probably be devoted to contestants who are on social security. Quiz shows allow the majority to see themselves on the screen. Their contestants are socially representative. This is very different from the quiz shows of the past two decades, which specialized in eccentric genius. It is not that present contestants know anything in particular, but that they know nothing at all. Their innocent materialism is intended to reflect the *affaire* between mass society and consumption. Questions are by design devoted to mass culture subjects; they deal with songs, celebrities, and movies. The whole point is that they constitute no obstacle to the mind. In fact, the current quiz show might better be described as a program anxious to *give* away money.

The rather nice young people who get showered with furniture, automobiles, and trips to Honolulu *deserve* this rain of manna on their heads. It has been awarded, not won. They are always young, and often black or female. They are pleasingly inarticulate and uneducated. They often cultivate a display of their own simplicity. Most important of all, they need what they are about to get.

Quiz shows which demand performance in more than one sense have become the genre of the decade. Contestants are lowest common denominators; the games they play are heavily influenced by random factors. The heart of their brief experience is exposure to a spinning roulette wheel or slot machine. There is no subject they can dominate — the machine indicates a new category every 30 seconds. The interesting thing, given their form, is that quiz shows are antiintellectual. For example, *Family Feud* accepts an answer only if it corresponds to what a selected group of other consumers think it is. It does no good to tick over facts about population, finances, or gross annual product when the question is about the most important city in California: If a majority of respondents have decided that they like San Francisco, then Los Angeles is wrong. Sometimes the redefinition of culture is not a metaphor.

In its consciously serious moments, programming attempts to deal with changes in the conception of rights and obligations. Local news shows are far less interested in the traditional subjects of news — politics and traffic accidents — than they are in the emergence of group identity. They now devote significant amounts of time and energy to locating constituencies and providing them with an audience. News is not what happens, it is how people feel about things.

Programming will often take gay rights or fat rights for equivalents of human rights. That is the way in which the latter become translated for mass society. There are emotional rights covered, for example, by programming about twins at a national sibling convention who argued that they were not given public credit for their "identity." The argument was not based on the traditional difficulty of recognizing two people who look alike. It was instead a much newer argument, that their personal demand upon society was not being met: Society was unprepared for the special emotional necessities of twins. It was as twins, not as mistaken individuals that they failed to get the emotional plenitude we all deserve. To understand this we must go through encounter, not through Erikson.

The assumption of local news or national documentaries is that aggrieved constituencies require the changing of social attitudes. Coverage of fat rights leads inexorably to the conclusion that fatness is really sexually attractive and that this should be widely understood. Or, that obesity is a matter of individual choice, so that its criticism is untoward. With each revelation of gay rights, vegetarian rights, or animal rights comes the suggestion that relativism is social change — or social progress. Some of the advice we get about obesity or vitamins or lesbianism is no doubt sound enough. But some of it is scientifically meaningless and morally incompetent. In providing a pretense of discourse, programming may be practicing medicine without a license.

Television deals directly rather than symbolically with social change on its celebrity talk shows. With the shift from print to image, and from production to consumption, a new class of savants has been given a social role. Celebrities once noted for success are now sources of opinion. Many of them are from the world of movies and television itself. Some have gone to China and others to Vietnam; some are known for their position on the environment and others for their activism against nuclear energy. A great many who are personally involved in therapies of various kinds become lobbyists for their causes.

Talk shows offer viewpoints on alcoholism, child care, mental illness, population control, and other issues bearing on social change. Celebrities appear in another incarnation on these shows: as mass society figures who are one or two degrees of consciousness ahead of their audience. In other words, mass culture has created its own moral and intellectual authority and does not really need to rely on the professionalized knowledge of high culture.

To sum up from the limited viewpoint of social change, televised "nonfiction" is the most literal of all genres. I have noted that quiz shows go so far as to exclude contestants who are elderly or even middle-aged; these shows believe only in demographic facts. Soft news programming invariably treats social change as a necessary consequence of personal or group grievances. But, while it identifies causes and constituencies, it manages also to translate their anxieties into entertainment. Televised "fiction" deals with social change in dramatic form. Feminism is implied by *Charlie's Angels* and the black bourgeoisie is depicted on *The Jeffersons*. The genre works indirectly because it must entertain. As for commercials, they are themselves symbolic and treat social change symbolically. They are bound body and soul to social change because every new commodity and each new purchase is a form of that. But commercials try to temper social change by their celebration of a viable social tradition. Almost alone in modern society they sing the praises of extinct social arrangements. They do so even while admitting that the goods and services they sell undermine those arrangements.

HOW COMMERCIALS SAY IT

There are two passages about the language of mass society that ought to be compared:

Style will frequently be fantastic, incorrect, overburdened, and loose, — almost always vehement and bold.
. . . There will be more wit than erudition, more imagina-

tion than profundity. . . . The object of authors will be to astonish rather than to please, and to stir the passions more than to charm the taste [de Tocqueville in Heffner, 1956: 177].

I was on *The David Susskind Show* with some [other] ad guys the other day, and he said, "Well, what is advertising supposed to do?" And one of them says, "It gives information." And that's really what most of them think it does, you know — take the good points, and present them to the people, and leave it to their good judgment. I mean, a lot of critics of advertising think we're all hustlers and charlatans; you kidding? They're not sharp enough to be good hustlers. Hustlers I love. . . . I told the guy, "You and I are in different businesses. I spray poison gas" [Price, 1978: 79-80].

The first passage is from de Tocqueville's account of language in a democracy. The second is from a copywriter, George Lois, exemplifying it. The language of advertising is that of Jacksonian democracy: It is not only as colorful as de Tocqueville foresaw but also direct, aggressive, exaggerated, and commonplace. Communication can be no more elementary. But that language is also symbolic, imagistic, allusive. Insofar as its intentions go, the metaphor of poison gas is appropriate.

The language of advertising is in some ways a language of concealment. It uses one word, *new,* more than any other in our hearing experience. But it moderates what is new or changing by applying it to the same commodity: Tide has been new annually for about a generation. Advertising insists on placing actually new products in a traditional social context: Commodities designed by computer and assembled by robots are sold by commercials placing them in quaint, wood-paneled general stores. They are praised by leathery Norman Rockwell types who would not know a chemical from a flat rock.

The word *new* refers to commodities but applies to experience. There is always the suggestion, which is true enough, that the novelty of the product corresponds to some liberating change in personal life. Sometimes the relationship becomes wonderfully contradictory, as when a brassiere, originally designed to restrain and confine, is said to offer freedom. I suppose that the idea of novelty could be Dichterized into almost any kind of interpretation, that it might represent eternal virginity or even the promise that Nick Carraway sees in the American frontier at the end of *The Great Gatsby*. From the viewpoint of social change its application is more simple: "New" commodities offer us equality in human progress. They do so by making each of us a customer of social change.

Perhaps one should say all of us, for the language of advertising is the ultimate of inclusiveness. One ITT commercial expresses the largest possible social intention when it states that "the best ideas are the ideas that help people." This says more than that the corporation wishes to make money or have itself praised. "People" is one of the great honorifics of our time. When ITT invokes the phrase it hopes, like General Motors, to resonate with majority aspirations. The object of "new" is "people." The desire to experience the former is legitimated by thought of the latter. Advertising rhetoric extends equality by emptying discourse of ideas and filling it with ideology. The average listener is reminded that what he hears, if not exactly *vox populi, vox dei,* is at least his own voice magnified 200 million times. The language of advertising — including the silent communication of its televised settings — deals in masses only; there are no individuals.

Is this to say that there are no individual dramatic characters on commercials? I suppose the answer to that is yes. The masses are identified by voice-overs referring to them as "boys," "girls," "baby," "Mom," "Pop," "you," and "we." They may occasionally have names, but not identities: Commercials are the *opposite* of drama. The fiction sustaining them is that we substitute our own characters for the personae invoked. When the speaker says "you," we think of ourselves; when he says "we," the vacuum is filled by thoughts of others known to us. In that way commercials draw us in to their company. "Baby" on diaper commercials is a blank space, to be filled by our perception of whatever baby is on our mind.

The language of advertising is full of inversion and innuendo. When commercials urge us to save, we know that we are meant to spend. We know that Water Pik, Noxema, and National Airlines make offers or propositions to us that do not have a great deal to do with showers, shaving, or trips to Miami Beach. We know that Xerox produces miracles, and that it is possible to lead very, very happy social lives by using the right cosmetic or pill. We know that consumption is the realm of what is truly, existentially "real," "exciting," and "good." But mass society gets other and more philosophical information from advertising. One example addresses itself to social conscience: Commercials now depict trios of man, woman, and black man or woman as the normative social unit. Children now come in assorted colors, and no beach party or shopping expedition is complete without its quota of minorities. This kind of visual inclusion speaks to equality and fulfills the intention of advertising to address the broadest possible public. It also reminds us of television's power of promoting doctrines of any kind. A second example has much less to do with social conscience and a good deal more to do with social pathology. We can now buy Luvs diapers, eat in Love's Restaurants, and buy a fully equipped Chevrolet Luv pickup truck. We stumble across the idea of "love" in almost every commercial that battens on our narcissism. There is a dark side to advertising, for it is willing to do anything not specifically prohibited by law or restrained, momentarily, by ethos. One reason why the dissolution of tradition is frightening is that advertising, the modern state, and other powers so easily fill up the empty spaces. The consumption of "love" means that society has been perceived by copy-writers — who are fairly far down the line of analysis from Spengler and Toynbee — as in some way vulnerable to a new *kind* of emotional appeal. Advertisements that used to sell satisfaction or pleasure are now selling something that mass society seems not to have: normal human relationships or the idea of them.

When de Tocqueville wrote that the language of democracy would "stir the passions," he evidently did not know the half of it. It is possible that sexuality discerned in advertising by Marcuse means less than the social aspects of emotional life. Marcuse rightly objected to the plastic nudity of advertisement, its continual suggestion that beauty and sexual pleasure were the rewards of commodities. It might now be argued that feelings about life are in a realm that ought not to be attached to commodities. To become sexually aroused by a shampoo seems less harmful than believing that social relationships are products of consumption or that advertising is a useful guide to a realm of sacred objects. But, of course, such an opinion is a cultural atavism or relic: Mass society inevitably draws all things within its orbit. The fundamental principle of mass language is that meaning must refer itself to the majority.

The language of advertising refers itself to social issues like affirmative action and to social conditions like the current reign of narcissism. In that way it keeps pace with other forms of media for whom change is itself a commodity. But how do commercials deal explicitly with social change? One way is simply to reiterate that their subject is "new." A second is to convey visual contexts, to suggest, for example, that outside the range of the speaker's voice there are women busy in authority. A third strategy is to symbolize change by having advice come from young to old: from daughters to mothers and from granddaughters to their grandmothers. A father buys a Buick because his son likes it, meaning that the decision has been based on superior technical knowledge — and in anticipation of old age, social uselessness, and death. On television, at least, out of the mouths of babes comes teleology.

There are two kinds of social change, aging, or the replacement of individuals, and progress, or the replacement of modes and institutions. Advertising connotes one when it denotes the other. When the Ford Motor Company praises "a new generation" of cars, the product implies the customer. In a society where the *only* physical ideal is youthfulness, the description is significant. The buyer is temporarily relieved of the sin of aging and becomes one with the "new generation." The same commercial insists that "it's happening now," which denotes a sale, but connotes the experience of life itself. Timeliness in advertising has a special meaning, referring not to actual need for commodities but to the state of mind induced by their possession. By getting that "new generation" automobile "right now" the consumer participates in society the only way he knows how. In this transaction, timeliness refers to social experience and novelty to the only authority known to mass culture and advertising, eternal youth.

There are then some fascinating differences between the medium and the message so far as commercials are concerned. Commercials are insistent and repetitious. They emphasize the sensate qualities of whatever it is that they sell, suggesting a garden of earthly delights. This leaves them very much open to the judgment of experience and of morality and to critical resentment. But criticism dwells too often on what it sees and says too little of what that means. The language of televised advertising has a consistent message to deliver about social life. It suggests not so much that consumption satisfies as that it participates in social change. It identifies change with perpetual youth; and by doing so makes some fairly momentous observations on American culture. The "philosophy" of this form of advertising is that all things are in flux. Dialectically, commercials envision society in the form of households and of steady employment. They depict man and nature in a working partnership. They even assimilate some of the more problematic issues of 20th-century life like new sexual identity and racial equality. But they do all this within a special context, in which aging and youth are in powerful opposition, in which "new" commodities symbolize new social arrangements. Whenever we look at a commercial we are looking at a modern morality playlet whose subject is the transcendence of things as they are. Of course, the original moralities had the advantage of a coherent religious system. We have only our desires, fed by the language of advertising, to change immediately while being forever the same.

NOTES

1. Wolfe (1978: 21-22) suggests that buying avant-garde art makes one "a fellow soldier, or at least an aide-de-camp or an honorary cong guerilla in the vanguard march through the land of the philistines." Avant-garde differentiates its consumer from "those Jaycees, those United Fund chairmen, those Young Presidents" who are the paradigm of middle-class success.

Advertising is a form of mass-cultural art that has moved on a track precisely opposite to that which, in going from Impressionism to Minimalism, has defined modern sensibility. The old realism, which advertising essentially is, is now by common criticial consent a form of Biedermayer or *Kitsch*. It is counterhistorical: With every plodding attempt to model recognizable human features, with every crystalline success at imaging half-melted ice-cream, the claims of advertising are diminished. Its mode is realism, which has been discredited for precisely the period of advertising's modern half-century.

2. The phrase is from Kierkegaard's essay "The Present Age."

3. The ad has been reproduced in its entirety in Berman (1980: 10).

5

ADVERTISING AND IMPOSED CHANGE

Advertising has to account for what it does, not only to sponsors and consumers but also to agencies of the federal government. How do those agencies arrive at their recommendations? And what are their conscious or unconscious visions of social change? The following chapter is about the imposition of change through federal regulation. It examines the recommendations of two federal agencies and concludes that they are based upon ideas that may not stand up to analysis. And it suggests ways in which it may be possible to identify the shifting tides and currents of social change.

THE INDUSTRY

The diversity of the advertising industry limits generalization about it. *Advertising Age* ("A look ahead . . . but no guarantees," 1980: 259-267) forecasts over $56 billion in advertising volume for 1980, with the largest amount going to newspapers and television and the rest to magazines, direct mail, business publications, transit systems, and billboards. Advertising agencies may not compare to ITT or General Motors, but they are genuine forms of big business: the billings of the top 25 range from J. Walter Thompson's annual figure of $764 million to the smaller but still impressive $83 million of Marsteller, Inc. These agencies employ thousands of writers, illustrators,

photographers, and executives and provide part-time jobs
for many actors, models, and musicians. They serve as
middlemen between manufacturers and the public and
between sponsors and media. There are necessarily great
differences between the individuals and institutions involved. Because of that, it is misleading to draw conclusions about common ideas or responsibilities.

We do not really know what "advertising" believes.
Our authority for what it may believe in part and from time
to time is provided by books from within the industry,
litigation between the industry and government, public
hearings, reports of the FTC and other agencies, marketing research, and journals like *Advertising Age*. But none
of these sources offers complete answers to two sets of
questions: one having to do with what the industry thinks
about itself, the other with what critics think about the
industry. As for the first, it would be useful to know answers to the following:

(1) Are there constituencies in the advertising industry
    which advocate social change?

(2) Does the advertising industry intentionally promote so-
    cial change in order to maximize profits?

(3) Or, does the industry perceive social change to interfere
    with its activity?

(4) To what extent do lobbies, critics, and government im-
    pose views of social change upon the industry?

(5) How does the industry lobby government?

(6) Are there certain books, values, or ideas about society
    that have special meaning for those in the advertising
    industry?

Until quantifiable information is available on these and
additional issues, any research into advertising's relationship to social change will be inexact.

Any answers that I have suggested must remain provisional. Probabilities will differ: It seems unlikely that any single book or ideology affects the social views of people in the industry. Like most businessmen, those in advertising do not have the time or inclination for reading. They tend, I think, to be indirectly influenced by ideas, which is to say that they come to positions in response to events. They become interested in the First Amendment rights of advertising, for example, as a result of litigation between the industry and the federal government.

There may be advocates of social change within the industry, but they are very well-disguised. Judging from newsletters and other publications, advertising's consciousness of social change seems much less focused than, say, that of the academic world. There seems to be either unanimity of outlook or indifference; I suspect the latter. Since advertising is very much an expanding industry, its energies are absorbed by growth. And, of course, the fact that it deals with literacy does not imply that it deals with ideas. It may be said that ideas reach copy writers and publicists long after they have been stated in either academic or public discourse.

Provisionally, I would say that social change is in fact perceived to be an obstacle to operations. Common experience and a reading of Max Weber convince us that all bureaucracies are reactionary. No institution willingly undergoes change. The changes caused by affirmative action — like putting women, hispanics, or blacks into commercials — mean additional effort and expense. It is understood that those changes must be undertaken without consulting the wishes of the agencies. A good deal of social change in the world of advertising is "compliance."

Advertising probably takes doctrines of feminism or personal liberation as they are already available in our culture from media or personal experience. It acknowledges and perhaps ratifies, but it does not originate social change. Its depiction of social life is probably also a form of "compliance" or acknowledgment of the realities and limits of our social discourse. It goes as far as it thinks it can without actual confrontation between opposed beliefs.

Advertising maneuvers between beliefs. In the world of commercials, present circumstances are made more tolerable by change: They are not outmoded. Commodities which may gratify or excite or liberate are marketed under the fiction that they reinforce family and community values. The ideal self of the consumer depicted by television is always changing through consumption, but never too much.

This endless maneuvering between change and stasis, past and present, liberation and tradition tends to escape criticism. We tend to invoke absolutes, to see advertising, like capitalism itself, as "a relentless engine of change, a revolutionary inflamer of appetites" (Will, 1980: C-2). A more useful analogy might be the political platform, which tries to make no enemies. Change is a mixed blessing in advertisements. The new authority of women is not easily worn; even those displaying it are ambiguous. Women in advertisements may have come a long way, but they are often depicted as mediating or even restraining social change.

THE CRITICS

Before critics or government agencies take their positions on advertising's responsibility for social change, they might ask these questions:

(1) What is a workable theory of social change?

(2) What constitutes evidence for advertising's success or failure at embodying social change?

(3) Is it realistic to expect advertising to do more than its normal amount of maneuvering among ideas, values, and interests?

A good deal of public argument has been undertaken without reference to these issues. One such argument, the FTC Report *Advertising and the Public Interest*, has been badly flawed by its failures in reasoning, evidence, and historical understanding. The economic changes that it recommends are based squarely upon a theory of social change:

> Another factor which as played an important role in changing consumer attitudes has been the questioning and searching re-examination of traditional values, a recent characterization [sic] of American society. Representative of these changes is the increased concern over the quality of the environment, the rights of minorities, and the problems of the poor.
>
> As a result of the pressures of expanding population, and the increased visibility of the by-products of a burgeoning technological society, Americans have recently become much more sensitive about environmental blight. . . . Activism over environmental issues is closely paralleled in the area of consumerism; and, taken together, they suggest that some rather fundamental changes in values are occurring. . . .
>
> Consumers are concerned with differential environmental impact of brand consumption, product safety, product durability, fairness of pricing practices, honesty of advertising appeals, and similar issues rather than availability or price. . . . These changes in values, when placed in historical perspective, may be viewed as ele-

ments in a shift of fundamental economic philosophy [Howard and Hulbert, 1973: 3].

At the risk of pedantry, this needs some close analysis. The statement is a theory of government intervention based upon social change, and the reader will naturally wish to judge its persuasiveness. Perhaps the following can serve as an outline for inquiry:

(1) In general, the invocation of environmentalism as an excuse for *any* kind of federal intervention has lost its impact since President Carter's 1978 announcement that the United States would reduce energy dependence by developing pollutant coal and nuclear resources. The "environment" is now one of a group of competing equities. It makes as much sense to address a theory of social change to unemployment or to cheap fuel as it does to rest on the unexamined virtues of "environmentalism."

(2) In general, "consumer" interests are no longer automatically identified with those of the FTC or other regulatory agencies. In fact, by 1980 the subject of congressional attack was not the advertising industry but the claims of the FTC to govern it. A movement still far from completion has begun to limit the powers of this agency.[1]

(3) Specifically, "environmentalism" and "consumerism" are not majority interests. To call them *values* is seriously to misrepresent what are really *causes*. There is no national majority impelled by these motives, although the media were for a time taken by them.

(4) It is unlikely that a majority of consumers are more interested in durability or in safety than they are in low prices. The report was published in 1973, just before the OPEC-caused inflation which has since made a joke of its assumptions. Those with discretionary income worry about issues; the majority worries about costs.

(5) Examination (and rejection) of traditional values was characteristic of the 1960s; but their reaffirmation has been characteristic of the late 1970s and early 1980s. The electorate has been conservative on issues like abortion, welfare, and the passage of ERA. All three candidates for the Presidency in 1980 were born-again Christians whose most devout feelings were directed at family sanctity. Although statistics now indicate that one family in every five is headed by someone single, separated, or divorced, the idea of the late Victorian or early modern family seemed remarkably appealing, at least in politics. Evidently, society is quite capable of responding to change by resisting it. If we base a theory of intervention upon one decade's enthusiasm for change, we may have to rewrite it because of another decade's enthusiasm for nostalgia.

(6) The Urban League and NAACP are generally recognized to speak with authority on the subject of our "increased concern" for the "rights of minorities and the problems of the poor." But, in 1980 the Directors of both organizations stated that the white majority had become far *less* interested in the disadvantaged than at any time in the past generation. They pointed out that there were now fewer jobs available for the uneducated, and that the large cities of the East needed more federal funds than they were getting. They noted the new national unwillingness to support welfare. They criticized the traditional allies of the disadvantaged in the Democratic Party for failing to support legislation for national programs of assistance. They cited evidence, in chapter and verse, that American social consciousness was changing in a way precisely opposite to that imagined by the FTC. In this respect, as in others, within a very few years of its publication (1973) the report has seen its assumptions invalidated.

What the report leaves out is as damaging as what it misinterprets. One of the most important changes on the social horizon has been the growth of evangelicalism, and all that it implies for our public values. Another major change has been the taxpayer's revolt which began with the passage of Proposition 13 in California. In the view of Peter Drucker, our foremost business analyst, there have been social changes even more important and even less visible to government. Drucker insists in his *Managing in Turbulent Times* that nothing — not OPEC or shortages of food or any other crisis — is as important for us to recognize as the "changes taking place in population structure and population dynamics" throughout the world (1980:75). These statistical changes mean that the developed world will be going through one kind of cultural change, and the undeveloped world a different but complementary change:

> The developed world. . . . will have to accept a sharp drop in the number of young people reaching working age; a sharp upgrading of schooling, and with it of expectations on the part of young people; an increasing heterogeneity of the labor force [1980: 94].

> In the developing countries, on the other hand, the overriding problem economically, socially, and politically will be to find jobs for a veritable tide of young people reaching working age — young people who are not very highly trained or very highly skilled but who are more highly trained and skilled than their parents were, have a much wider horizon if only because of radio and television, who know how the rich world lives [1980: 95].

Advertising and the Public Interest assumed that "fundamental changes in values are occurring" which would lead to "a shift of fundamental economic philosophy." But it seems that the report expected a new cultural dispensation that never arrived, and that it did not notice the one that did.

No theory of social change was required necessary role of government. Truth in always be desirable, and to the credit of was a central recommendation. But no am cation about social change can justify its other recom mendations: for example, that a program of public meetings should begin in order to expound the views of social life adopted by the authors. These meetings were to be earnestly philosophical, to communicate "the receptivity to new ideas that we have seen among members of the staff" (Howard and Hulbert, 1973: 90). I think that a fair translation of this is that the staff members, like many in the federal bureaucracy, had their social conscience stimulated by ideas new to them, ideas they felt all right-thinking people ought to have. In a culture always on the watch for something new, they wished to participate in progress. They wished to share the moral respectability of environmentalism and the intellectual respectability of "fundamental changes in values." And, more than anything else, they wished to inform a national audience of middle-class people very like themselves of their conversion to saving ideas. There is a religious analogy here, better left unpursued.

Other recommendations indicate a central confusion, that between values and interests. After a long discussion of the psychology of consumption the report concluded that the FTC was empowered to oversee the "attitude," "confidence," "power," and "self-concept" of the American consumer. The authors realized that they were edging into unknown territory but did not realize quite how dangerous it might be. They urged that consumers had to be psychologically satisfied by their purchases. They believed that those purchases had to be rationally decided. And they argued that manufacturers and advertisers were obliged to design and market products commensurate with these obligations.

is impossible here to go over all the psychological octrine that ought to serve as a context for this. Suffice it to say that modern psychology will not provide an apologetic for any theory which assumes that desires are rational or that satisfactions proceed from our intentions. The supposed obligation to support the "confidence" and define the "attitude" of the consumer does not refer, actually, to psychology. These terms are subideas lifted from the literature of self-realization. To invoke them is to moralize.

The report is precisely *not* being psychological when it asserts that consumers are helpless before the persuasive powers of advertising; or that all of us are baffled and alienated by industrial society; or that people react fearfully to new encounters; or that they are defenseless in the marketplace; or that consumption is a matter of "personal attitudes" rather than transactions. Most difficult of all to believe is that the end of every transaction is to become objectively satisfied with commodities and with ourselves. When the FTC invokes these ideas it makes two assumptions, neither of which is convincing. The first is that customers and the marketplace have an adversary relationship. Let the buyer beware not only of individual commodities which may deceive his judgment but also of an entire system of marketing designed to entrap him. The second assumption is that human nature is adequately described by an extremely narrow set of doctrines taken from the general theory of alienation. To be guided by those doctrines is to believe that individuals have also an adversary relationship with all of society.

Advertising and the Public Interest ought to be evaluated by the ground it has taken. Its excursions into public morality, social change, and psychology seem not to have added to its economic analysis. It may be, in fact, that its recommendations are based upon social ideas that are incompetent.

ADVERTISING AND RIGHTS

A second case involves the U.S. Commission on Civil Rights, which has made its own recommendations on changes that ought to be imposed upon advertising and the programming that it supports. The commission has published two reports: *Window Dressing on the Set: Women and Minorities in Television* and *Window Dressing on the Set: An Update*. Both agree that television "does not reflect the sexual and racial/ethnic make-up of the United States" (U.S. Commission on Civil Rights, 1977: 148). The criterion is social reality, things as they actually are. Judged by that criterion, white males are overrepresented on television while females and minorities are insufficiently visible. It is important, even crucial, to see how this standard becomes translated into its opposite.

"Stereotyping" is defined by both *Window Dressing* reports as the depiction of characters in ways that *do not* reflect social reality. If, for example, women now make up about half the national working force, that new social fact should be recognized by having them make up about half the working force on televised drama. But the commission wishes also to have "stereotyping" mean an offense against ideals. It objects to precisely those aspects of television which *do* represent social actuality: the depiction of men holding most positions of authority at work, the depiction of many women as housewives, the depiction of minorities in subordinate economic roles. In short, "stereotyping" not only means that television should conform to social facts but also means that it should depict society as the commission would like to have it exist. The contradiction is never resolved by these reports. Television is consistently accused of not showing the world as it is — and of not showing the world as it should be.

The commission makes more than one logical contradiction. "Actual" social conditions are much worse than they are depicted on television. They are much less fair to our ideals. In actuality, a horrifying percentage of black males are unemployed. In actuality, about half the crimes committed in our cities are committed by blacks, against black victims. In actuality, too many of the conditions depicted by *The Moynihan Report* still exist. If television were morally bound to depict statistical actuality, then it would have to dramatize these uncongenial facts. But we all know that it does not, and we are grateful for it. Instead, *all* actuality on television is a kind of fiction. The commission is not displeased because television is insufficiently factual — it is displeased with the kind of fiction television has chosen.

Is the commission a competent judge of fiction? Not if we are to judge from its analysis of television history. Two points recur again and again, the first having to do with the nature of fiction as a genre. The commission, like the Soviet Ministry of Culture, believes that fiction should support orthodoxies. It believes that the role of fiction is to carry social messages in dramatic form. Comedy and drama are to be judged by the approved social goods they promote. After expressing enormous displeasure with these genres, the commission explains their real function in a good society:

> "All in the Family" has treated such topics as compulsive gambling, menopause, breast cancer, aging, death, and rape. "Maude" has explored alcoholism, white liberalism, mental health, abortion, and changing sex roles. "Good Times" has dealt with venereal disease, hypertension, equal employment opportunity, and ghetto ripoffs [U.S. Commission on Civil Rights, 1977: 20].

The commission is especially pleased that information about breast cancer reached 40 million viewers after Edith

Bunker suffered from it; that the Population Institute contributed ideas about "parenting" to *All in the Family*; that
there was a significant rise in the number of voluntary
requests for blood pressure checks after a character on
Good Times suffered from hypertension; and that Archie
Bunker's decision to donate blood resulted in increased
business for the Red Cross throughout the nation.

Aside from the fact that the commission consigns
white liberalism to a place between alcoholism and
neurosis, there remain two things to be said. The first is
that drama is responsible only for itself. Since the decision
to allow *Ulysses* into the United States a half century ago,
it has been accepted by both law and literary criticism that
fiction does not need to conform to particular moral
views. And, since the start of operation of ministries of
culture throughout the Communist world, we have seen
how easy it is to censor in the guise of providing good
advice. As far as literature goes, the idea that stories are
justified by their public morality is as dead as the dodo.
The commission demands what entertainment cannot
give: a coherent world view and an image of social life
completely ego-stabilized. The ideal show would be
guided not only by affirmative action but also by the requirements to take X-rays, diet, check our blood pressure,
and avoid littering the streets. Televised drama is mass
culture art and perhaps deserves to be criticized on the
grounds of its triviality. But it does not deserve to be
censored because federal bureaucrats believe that the
role of comedy is to promote pleasing ideas.

The second reason is unwittingly provided by the
commission itself. After noting that various constituencies
now maintain regular contact with the producers of television drama, and that they "assist" them to change their
scripts so that ideas, causes, or minorities will be shown

to advantage, the commission innocently notes the following:

> Norman Lear employs an assistant, Virginia Carter, who works with public interest groups, listening to their suggestions as well as their complaints.
>
> According to Mindy Beck, in her article on "Minority Images on TV," Lear's "open-door policy" *has not satisfied everybody*. Charles Cook, West Coast regional director for the Congress of Racial Equality (CORE), describes his relationship with Tandem Productions as a "state of cold war." He criticizes Ms. Carter for providing coffee *but no solutions* to what CORE believes are programs which perpetuate black stereotypes. Cook thinks that there has been little change and that none is forthcoming as long as Lear's product continues to be profitable [U.S. Commission on Civil Rights, 1977: 24; emphasis added].

The commission has provided its own conclusive argument against its own theory, but fails to see it. It means by the above that Lear has not done his job: which is to satisfy public morality, CORE, and the authors of the report. It does not ask whether or not CORE should be "advising" or censoring Tandem Productions; whether Tandem is obliged to come up with solutions to problems that society itself has failed to attain; or whether Tandem and Norman Lear should stop working for profit.

The commission has failed to ask the obvious question: What happens, in a world of diminishing returns, when even the best-intentioned efforts to promote social change prove unsatisfactory? What if Lear had sincerely tried to please everyone and failed? Is it possible that *nothing* Tandem can do will please public morality; that, in fact, public morality is so divided up among so many constituencies that to please one will enrage the other? Censorship in general fails not because it is ineffective but because it is infinitely extensible. *Huckleberry Finn*, once censored by reaction for its immorality, was afterward censored by reform for its portrayal of Nigger Jim. Censorship can eventually be satisfied only by the blank and unwritten page.

CRITICISM: OBJECTIVE AND OTHERWISE

Any serious scholarly work in the future will want to take into consideration matters asserted and evaded by federal agencies intent on basing intervention upon theories of social change. The first will probably be the matter of interpretation. Is there a *correct* reading of televised drama or even of commercials? One of the conclusions of modern literary criticism has been that no single explanation can exhaust meaning. A line of poetry is what it means — but it also means more than can be said about it. A corollary is that more than one correct statement can be made about it. Is it true, to turn to the lesser case of television, that a woman depicted as a housewife has no "authority?" Is she without emotional or moral authority? Is she without the authority based upon respect or superior knowledge or character? Is a housewife by definition inferior to a lawyer? To interpret the history of televised drama by counting only roles of formal authority — as the Commission on Civil Rights does — is to lose track of the possibility that Lucille Ball showed her "authority" or power over home, husband, and social circumstances in ways that the machine of government seems never to have enjoyed.

Is it necessary for restraints to be imposed upon commercials and programming in order to avoid "potential harm" to those who see themselves *generically* represented on screen without more social power than they actually possess? Do all women identify with women on screen? Can the same be said for age, race, class, or occupation? It is actually fairly simpleminded to believe that the viewer responds only to what a bureaucrat believes is his generic self-conception. There are other issues involved: for example, is the idea of "potential harm" intellectually meaningful? Does the Commission on Civil Rights, which would restrict the power of television to portray character in a way displeasing to constituents or to itself, have an adequate idea about potentiality, harm, or human nature? Possibly it cannot distinguish between harm and resentment. And, it may be ascribing its own motives to the viewer.

The only way, eventually, of avoiding "potential harm" to any viewer is to broadcast only those things that show all constituencies of age, race, or sex favorably in every respect. It is not especially that this makes *The Merchant of Venice* unplayable, but that it is psychologically false. And, of course, to do so would completely reinvent the idea of the "stereotype."

It may be that the FTC and the Commission on Civil Rights offer us opinions about American society disguised as discussions of media. For example, the commission finds, to its distress, that television reflects the actualities of life, presenting "a social structure in which males are very much in control." It observes that male characters lead lives more diverse than females and have more prestigious occupations. When it criticizes television for showing life in this way it convicts the medium only of accuracy. It implies that the depiction of our social order is unjust rather than imprecise.

Scholarship has been deeply concerned by the relationship between sponsors and programming. The basic question is the relationship of expression of ideas to the power of financial control. In reviewing this connection Herbert J. Gans in *Deciding What's News* and Martin Seiden in *Who Controls the Mass Media* have concluded that the affect of advertisers' prejudices on programming is minimal (see, e.g., Gans, 1979: 249-278).[2] Can government arrogate a privilege that sponsors do not and should not have, of requiring commercials and programs to carry "approved" social ideas?

It might be noted that both the FTC and the commission deal with the same broad subjects as the National Endowment for the Arts and the National Endowment for the Humanities. Can they act differently from these agencies in regard to the control of expression? It is understood by both of these endowments and by the congressional committees overseeing them that the government does not have the right to demand conformity even when it pays directly for the expression of ideas. Their understanding is that the government is not a literary critic. When critics write about the flaws of programs or commercials, they exercise the right of absolute diversity. They can demand *anything* of their subject. When government takes on the role of critic, it asks only for *one* thing: compliance. This is the opposite of critical dialogue. In order for a federal agency to operate, it must espouse a single point of view. It must act, in cases dealing with expression, as if it were a judiciary of the mind. That is exactly what this country does not need.

Is the government a reliable social critic? When the FTC tried to identify the most important social changes of our time it left out inflation, the liberation of women, the shrinking population of the developed world and the exploding population of the undeveloped world, the incredible rise of evangelicalism, and the revolt of Californian and other taxpayers against big government. To compound the error, by identifying environmentalism and consumerism as the wave of the future, the FTC confused public values with the momentary interests of its staff members. The FTC defined regulation as part of consumerism and then defined consumerism as a new public value. In effect, it suggested that what it did constituted desirable social change.

The FTC report put away consumer motives of the dead social past like low prices, general availability of products, and the satisfaction of demand. It adopted the view that we have become different from other generations, demanding of the market only that goods be rational, beneficial, and harmless to nature. This forcibly suggests that government has limited areas of competence.

After reading dozens of books attacking advertising because it represents capitalism, productivity, and materialism, the reader is left with a sense of argumentative pleasure. Marcuse and Galbraith may be wrong but they know how to think. They have been able to identify many serious issues of modern life, and they have the intellectual power to work their way through contradictions. As a result of reading *Advertising and the Public Interest* or *Window Dressing on the Set*, the reader is left with a sense of depression. These reports derive their ideas from what Dwight Macdonald called "midcult," that exceedingly gray area between mass culture and high culture, in which things are simplified for educated ignorance. In these reports we see Sunday-supplement analysis of alienation, self-realization, and all the rights we seem to have against each other.

The reports are short on economic analysis with the Civil Rights Commission going so far as to suggest that one of the faults of Norman Lear's productions is that they run for a profit. The reports rely on unconvincing evidence. I have mentioned (Chapter 2) the large body of material published in the *Journal of Communication* which suffers from two kinds of bias: that of taking its very limited findings for universals and that of infusing research with ideology. This kind of research is quite capable of interpreting a pie in the face as either an offense against dignity or the opening hostilities of World War III. It discusses sexism from the point of view of lobbyists. It suggests darkly that ours is not only a profit-seeking but also a fascist economy, in which consumers are threatened by violence on the screen so that they will obey established powers. The point of this kind of research is not that it comes up with new facts, but that it subordinates facts to convictions. The two *Window Dressing* reports cite the same evidence on social control that I have described without admitting that other studies disagree with their interpretation (see Cater and Strickland, 1975: 73-76; 85-87; 135). One of the biggest problems facing any commission is its own willingness to adapt evidence to circumstances.

To judge from these two cases, the relationship between government and advertising is affected by the reasoning brought to bear on evidence. Certain forms of behavioristic research count the scenes of comedy or of horse-opera in order to determine the social power of young against old, black against white, and of male against female. When government accepts such formulas, it unconsciously agrees that all human relationships are adversary relationships. When government criticizes commercials for their social content, it disregards the eternal requirements of drama, that actions occur within a plot. The bureaucrat, like the behaviorist, becomes responsive only to a single idea. He objects to housewives sexually ecstatic over a box of soap not because the idea is laughable but because washing clothes for others is demeaning.

Of course, advertising can be free neither from criticism nor from the ministrations of government. But those who speak in the name of the public do not always represent it. A clear distinction has to be made between criticism founded on evidence and criticism founded on ideology.

Advertising has been caught up in a situation larger than is generally realized, even within the industry. As the voice of technology, advertising is associated with many dissatisfactions of industrial life. It courts dissatisfaction because it relies so heavily on the institutions of everyday life. If it does not succeed in its promise to make us happy, is it not responsible for our unhappiness? As the voice of mass culture, advertising addresses itself relentlessly to the majority. Because of that it invites intellectual contempt. Its morality is consumption and its art form is realism — primitive modes in a sophisticated society. Because of its connection with television, advertising invites the attention of government. And because government must reduce all complexities to the simplifications of policy, it can perceive advertising in only one way: insofar as it fails or succeeds in depicting particular ends. Finally, advertising is an irresistible target for constituencies, of which there are many. Those with visions of social change are drawn to advertising because it seems able to do so much about them — and they are drawn to government, which seems able to do so much about controlling advertising. They see advertising as an instrument of history, able to bring about or prevent change. They judge it by its social morality, diffused into a thousand visions of perfection. The democratic marketplace has until now been able to contain contradictions; it remains to be seen whether it can do the same with the little forms of absolutism.

NOTES

1. See especially Gellhorn (1980). Gellhorn observes that "the commission was caught in a shift of public attitude away from consumerism and the use of government to protect consumers" (p. 40). It is an odd fate for an agency which justified its activities by a theory of social change.

2. According to Gans (1979: 253) evening news programs and news-magazines are "virtually free" of pressure from advertisers. Gans lists other sources of censorship, however: from affiliate stations, government, interest groups, lobbies, and peers within journalism.

REFERENCES

"A look ahead . . . but no guarantees" (1980) Advertising Age (April 30): 259-267.

ARNOLD, M. (1962) "Democracy," in L. Trilling (ed.), The Portable Matthew Arnold. Baltimore: Penguin.

BELL, D. (1976) The Cultural Contradictions of Capitalism. New York: Basic Books.

BERMAN, R. (1980) "Advertising and Social Change." Twentieth Century Advertising and the Economy of Abundance. Chicago: Crain.

BERMAN, R. (1979) "Art vs. the arts." Commentary (November): 48.

BERMAN, R. (1968) America in the Sixties. New York: Free Press.

BOORSTIN, D. J. (1973) The Americans: The Democratic Experience. New York: Random House.

BOURNE, R. (1920) History of a Literary Radical and Other Essays. New York: Biblo and Tanner.

BRAUDEL, F. (1973) Capitalism and Material Life 1400-1800. New York: Harper & Row.

BURNHAM, W. D. (1980) "Review of The Pulse of Politics." New Republic (May 24): 30.

CATER, D. and S. STRICKLAND (1975) TV Violence and the Child. New York: Russell Sage Foundation.

CRANE, H. (1970) The Bridge. New York: Liveright.

DeFLEUR, M. L. (1964) "Occupational roles as portrayed on television." Public Opinion Quarterly 28: 71.

DICHTER, E. (1975) Packaging: The Sixth Sense? Boston: Houghton-Mifflin.

DRUCKER, P. (1980) Managing in Turbulent Times. New York: Harper & Row.

DRUCKER, P. (1978) The Age of Discontinuity: Guidelines to Our Changing Society. New York: Harper & Row.

"Editorial" (1978) Wall Street Journal (June 19).

ELIOT, T. S. (1950) Selected Essays. New York: Harcourt Brace Jovanovich.

EVANS, J. (1969) Life in Medieval France. New York: Macmillan.

EWEN, S. (1976) Captains of Consciousness. New York: McGraw-Hill.

FITZGERALD, F. S. (1953) The Great Gatsby. New York: Scribner's.

FREUD, S. (1961) Civilization and Its Discontents. New York: W. W. Norton.

GALBRAITH, J. K. (1976) The Affluent Society. New York: New American Library.

GALBRAITH, J.K. (1973) Economics and the Public Purpose. Boston: Houghton-Mifflin.

GALBRAITH, J.K. (1971) The New Industrial State. Boston: Houghton-Mifflin.

GANS, H.J. (1979) Deciding What's News. New York: Pantheon.

GELLHORN, E. (1980) "The wages of zealotry: The FTC under siege." Regulation (January/February): 33-40.

GERBNER, G. and L. GROSS (1976) "Living with television: The violence profile." Journal of Communication (spring): 182.

GERBNER, G., L. GROSS, M. JACKSON-BEECK, S. JEFFRIES-FOX, and N. SIG-NORIELLI (1978) "Cultural indicators: Violence profile no. 9." Journal of Communication (summer): 176-207.

GIES, J. and F. GIES (1973) Life in a Medieval City. New York: Crowell.

HALLER, J.S. and R.M. HALLER (1977) The Physician and Sexuality in Victorian America. New York: W.W. Norton.

HEFFNER, R.D. [ed.] (1956) Democracy in America. New York: New American Library.

HOWARD, J.A. and J. HULBERT (1973) Advertising and the Public Interest. New York: American Marketing.

HUTCHINSON, T. [ed.] (1953) The Poetical Works of Wordsworth. New York: Oxford University Press.

HYMAN, S.E. (1962) The Tangled Bank. New York: Macmillan.

JANOWITZ, M. (1978) The Last Half-Century. Chicago: University of Chicago Press.

JONSON, B. (1967) Volpone. New Haven, CT: Yale University Press.

JONSON, B. (1963) Ben Jonson: Three Plays. New York: W.W. Norton.

KEATS, J. (1899) The Complete Poetical Works and Letters of John Keats. Cambridge, MA: Harvard University Press.

KENNER, H. (1975) A Homemade World. New York: Morrow.

KITTREDGE, G.L. [ed.] (1936) The Complete Works of Shakespeare. New York: Ginn and Company.

KNIGHTS, L.C. (1937) Drama and Society in the Age of Jonson. London: Macmillan.

LANG, J.S. (1979) "Madison Avenue takes on Washington." U.S. News and World Report (June 18): 31.

LASCH, C. (1978) The Culture of Narcissism. New York: W.W. Norton.

LATTIMORE, R. (1959) The Complete Greek Tragedies (Vol. 3). Chicago: University of Chicago Press.

LEISS, W. (1976) The Limits of Satisfaction. Toronto: Toronto University Press.

LEYMORE, V.L. (1975) Hidden Myth. New York: Basic Books.

LICHINE, A. (1973) Encyclopedia of Wines & Spirits. New York: Knopf.

LIPSET, S.M. and R. BENDIX (1967) Social Mobility in Industrial Society. Berkeley: University of California Press.

MACDONALD, D. (1961) Masscult and Midcult. New York: Partisan Review.

MARCUSE, H. (1964) One-Dimensional Man. Boston: Beacon Press.

MITCHELL, A. and I. DEAK (1974) Everyman in Europe: Essays in Social History, the Preindustrial Millenia. Englewood Cliffs, NJ: Prentice-Hall.

MOTT, F.L. (1962) American Journalism. New York: Macmillan.

NELSON, P. (1974) "The economic value of advertising," pp. 56-57 in Y. Brozen (ed.), Advertising and Society. New York: Harper & Row.

NICOSIA, F.M. (1974) "Advertising and the manipulation of consumers," pp. 244-281 in Advertising, Management, and Society. New York: Harper & Row.

O'DONNELL, W.J. and K.J. O'DONNELL (1978) "Update: Sex-role messages in TV commercials." Journal of Communication (winter): 156-158.

O'KELLY, C.G. and L.E. BLOOMQUIST (1976) "Women and blacks on TV." Journal of Communication (autumn): 179-184.

"Opinion roundup" (1979a) Public Opinion (June/July).

"Opinion roundup" (1979b) Public Opinion (March/May).

Oxford University (1970) The Oxford Illustrated Dickens. New York: Oxford University Press.

PLUMB, J.H. (1965) The Italian Renaissance: A Concise Survey of Its History and Culture. New York: Harper & Row.

POWER, E. (1963) Medieval People. New York: B & N.

PRICE, J. (1978) The Best Thing on TV. New York: Viking.

"The 'punk rock' scene turns to bloody violence." San Diego Union (July 11): A-18.

SCHUMPETER, J.A. (1975) Capitalism, Socialism and Democracy. New York: Harper & Row.

SHILS, E. (1975) Center and Periphery. Chicago: University of Chicago Press.

SKOLNICK, A. (1980) "The paradox of perfection." Wilson Quarterly (summer): 119.

SOMERVELL, D.C. [ed.] (1971) A Study of History by Arnold Toynbee (Vol. 1, abridged). New York: Dell.

STANFIELD, J.R. (1979) Economic Thought and Social Change. Carbondale: Southern Illinois University Press.

STEIN, B. (1980) The View from Sunset Boulevard. New York: Doubleday.

TRILLING, L. (1973) Sincerity and Authenticity. Cambridge, MA: Harvard University Press.

TRILLING, L. (1972) Mind in the Modern World. New York: Viking.

TRILLING, L. (1950) The Liberal Imagination. New York: Viking.

TWAIN, M. (1962) Huckleberry Finn. New York: W.W. Norton.

U.S. Commission on Civil Rights (1977) Window Dressing on the Set: Women and Minorities in Television. Washington, DC: Government Printing Office.

U.S. Department of Commerce (1977) Social Indicators 1976. Washington, DC: Government Printing Office.

VAN DEN HAAG, E. (1961) "A dissent from the consensual society," p. 59 in N. Jacobs and P. Lazarsfeld (eds.), Culture for the millions? Princeton, NJ: Princeton University Press.

WARREN, D. (1978) "Commercial liberation." Journal of Communication (winter): 171.

WATTENBERG, B.J. (1976) The Real America. New York: Capricorn.

WESTOVER, T. (1980) "One fray at a time." TV Guide (May 10-16): 28.

WHITE, T.H. (1978) In Search of History. New York: Warner Books.

WILL, G. (1980) "But the issue *is* bread and butter." *San Diego Union* (August 24): C-2.

WILSON, E. (1950) Classics and Commercials. New York: Noonday.

WOLFE, T. (1978) The Painted Word. New York: Bantam.

INDEX

INDEX

ABOUT THE AUTHOR

RONALD BERMAN holds an A.B. in Social Relations from Harvard and a Ph.D. in English from Yale. Among his previous works are *A Reader's Guide to Shakespeare's Plays* and *America in the Sixties: An Intellectual History.* He was Chairman of the National Endowment for the Humanities from 1971 to 1977.